Tax Updates: Trump Tax to Coronavirus

A detailed summary of tax law changes from the Tax Cuts and Jobs Act through the various Coronavirus stimulus bills

Kirk Taylor

Copyright 2020-2021 Kirk Taylor

To the extent that this book uses specific numbers, they are for the 2020 tax year (tax returns filed in Jan – April of 2021). I will update periodically, and significant changes can be followed on my tax blog: www.supertaxgenius.com

**January 2021 Update**: This is the fourth major update to the book and, as a result, things have gotten a bit clunky. For that reason, I have added a chapter immediately after this introduction that includes a full summary of the very latest change (the $600 stimulus bill). It also includes a discussion of how those changes will be incorporated into the various sections to try to eliminate confusion and make the book easier to read. If you were planning on skipping around and looking for just the things that apply to you, make sure to read this first new section.

**Now here is the original start of the book:**

So much has changed in the tax world in the last few years, that I decided a nice, compact and easy to read summary was in order. This book will start with a basic tax law primer and discussion of various terms, to ensure we are on the same page, and then describe how the various laws changed the way taxes work. I am going to write the book in English, vice Taxese, so you can understand not just what the changes say, but how they impact your life. As with most of my shorter tax books, I will try to organize things such that the most important or universally applicable stuff comes first, and more esoteric stuff comes later. I am also going to include some things that have nothing to do with tax law changes, mainly really important, simple advice that most people should be following.

The target audience for this book are people who file Form 1040 and 1040SR (formerly 1040, 1040A and 1040EZ). There are a few things in here for C and S Corporations, Partnerships and trusts, but those aren't the focus. If your business is filed with your regular tax return (on Schedule C) this book is for you. I also do not cover details of HAVING employees, though I mention a few things.

This update (the fourth) is being written in December of 2020, to be published in January 2021. This is well after the first round of stimulus checks have been sent to most people. The CARES Act has been law for many months and much of the details have been worked out. Forms for the 2020 tax year are written and in final review. A Payroll tax holiday was put forth as an Executive Order. I expect more laws to be passed, and I will include them if they come out before publishing, and I will update periodically. In order to ensure that you don't have to keep buying new versions of this book, I will provide expanded information on my blog, www.supertaxgenius.com for free. I will eventually start over with a new book, once a new administration comes into power, or they have a big tax law change that does not have anything to do with Coronavirus or post Coronavirus stimulus.

At the time of publishing, the politicians were arguing about another set of $2000 stimulus checks, or an extra $1400 on top of the $600 that most people should have by the end of January. If all they do is up the money, I won't bother to update the book, as you will get everything you need to know from the news, and you can be fairly confident that they will just dump the extra money in the same place they dumped your $600 (if you were eligible).

This book contains my very unvarnished, very uncensored opinions. Some of the information in this book has been previously published in one form or another in some of my other books but has been reviewed, updated and adjusted as necessary to be more useful and timely in this book.

For the entirety of this book, I am going to refer to Economic Impact Payments as stimulus payments, since that's what most people are referring to them as. We are talking about the $1200 per person money that started arriving April 15th, and the $600 payments in January of 2021. I also will generally refer to bills with slang titles like Trump Tax Law and Coronavirus Tax or CARES Tax, vice the ridiculous titles the bills are given. Some tax changes are slipped into non-tax bills, in which case I will simply mention what years they apply to, rather than specifying where they came from.

None of this book is meant to be political in nature, and, if it seems like I am taking a partisan slant, that is not the case. I will occasionally mock politicians, the Internal Revenue Service (IRS), other government agencies and even various Presidents, but it is just good-natured mocking of the bosses, and not meant as a partisan political statement.

If you find this book useful, you should consider at least two of my other books: <u>The Short Cheap Tax Book for Everyone</u> and <u>Everyday Taxes</u>. Make sure to get the latest year of Everyday Taxes, which is normally published in June. The Short Cheap Tax Book has almost universally applicable great advice, and Everyday Taxes has dozens of chapters ordered around life events. The first is cheap, the second quite a bit more expensive because it has detailed information and takes months to write – so you're paying for the damage to my two typing fingers. That's right, everything in the books and on the blogs is written by a hunt and pecker. There are also several more specific Short Cheap Tax Books, including one for students and another for the military.

One last favor…reviews are the lifeblood of a self-published author. If this book didn't meet your expectations, or you don't feel you got your money's worth, or the book didn't provide you an answer you were looking for, please reach out to me before dropping a one-star review. I value the feedback and am always trying to make my books better. You can reach me through my aforementioned blog. If you love the book, or it saved you money, please drop a good review on Amazon. Thanks!

DISCLAIMER:

Because lawyers suck and people are greedy, it is important to point out that this book represents MY opinions and interpretations and are not necessarily those of the IRS or my employer. These chapters are translated into basic English, and are distilled down to the most important points, so they may not cover all details and may not be accurate for your situation. Do your own research to be certain. Talk to a competent professional. Do not rely solely on this book. Also, client confidentiality is important, so the spirit of client stories is true, but the details are significantly altered. Also, to be clear, I am neither a currently licensed financial advisor, nor a mental health counselor of any kind.

All links were functional and directed to the correct web page at the time the book is published. I cannot be held responsible for the IRS or other agencies rejiggering their websites around. Most of the pages referenced can be found with a simple Google search using the main page as part of the search. For example, you might enter the following on Google to find the new W-4 form: "irs.gov W-4". It is usually more effective to use Google rather than a website's own search tools, especially with the IRS and other large or popular websites.

# The Latest COVID Relief Bill (Dec 2020)

This is the bill with the $600 stimulus checks.

This bill had a lot of tax provisions that aren't getting a lot of attention. They also overlap, change or eliminate a lot of stuff that was in the original Trump Tax Bill and CARES Act. In past updates I had mostly included the new rules alongside the old rules, or with an UPDATE section in the midst of the chapters, leaving the old stuff in place. This has caused things to get a bit cluttered, especially in the disaster relief sections.

For that reason, I am going to try to just overwrite most of the no longer relevant information, rather than updating alongside old stuff.

Speaking of important information, the latest bill made two changes that allow you to use 2019 numbers to calculate 2020 tax results. I'll cover these later, but the big, HUGE, really IMPORTANT thing is that you need to make sure your 2019 information is available and used by whatever method you choose to do your 2020 taxes. If you use the same software or preparer, it SHOULD automatically calculate the best way to use your 2019 information, but you should check to be certain. If you use new software, it should ask you for 2019 information and you want to make sure you have your 2019 return available when preparing your 2020 return. If you use a professional preparer, provide them a printout of your 2019 tax return so they can pull any information they need – this is good advice every year.

## The New Stimulus Check:

The amounts for this are $600 for each adult individual (meaning a married couple filing jointly gets $1200) as well as dependents age 16 or under as of 2019. The rules are almost exactly the same as the previous checks, which are covered in great detail in the later chapter on the subject. Here I am going to cover things in a lot less detail, highlighting the major differences.

First, if the place your first stimulus went is still active, the new stimulus should go there, and you don't need to take any action. If it is not still open, you can update it at irs.gov using the big "Get My Economic Impact Payment" button. The button doesn't do much right now since they are still programming for the new payment, but it should be soon.

Payments are based on 2019 tax returns, social security or VA disability information for non-filers, or information you provided for the previous $1200 payments. They are tax free advances on your 2020 taxes and will be recalculated when you file your 2020 tax return, and any additional money you are due will be provided then, but no repayment is due if you would have been entitled to less.

I highly recommend e-filing a 2020 tax return, using direct deposit if possible, to make sure you get everything you are entitled to, and to keep your information with the IRS as up to date as possible. Who knows, they may want to send more money! I think this is one of the enduring tax lessons from the pandemic – file a tax return even when not required.

The income limitations for the new stimulus payments were slightly modified from the previous ones. The phaseout starts at the same point, but the payments go down faster as your income goes up. Phaseout starts at $75,000 for Single and Married Filing Separate (MFS) filers, $112,500 for Head of Household (HH), and $150,000 for Married Filing Joint and Qualified Widowers (MFJ/QW). If your income is below those numbers, you should get a full payment. Single and MFS filers get nothing once income hits $87,000 and MFJ/QW filers get nothing when income hits $174,000. HH goes away at $124,000.

You can find Additional details and actions for weird situations can be found in the later chapter from the original round of stimulus checks.

# The Rest of the Tax Changes (from the latest bill):

This is a broad overview of the rule changes. More details are provided in relevant chapters if necessary.

1. **Charity**: You can deduct up to $300 in cash contributions to charity on 2020 even if you don't normally itemize. Cash means cash/check/credit but not donation of things or time. There is a penalty of 20% of taxes for cheating on this. For 2021 the limit is $600 and the penalty 50%. You can also donate up to 100% of your Adjusted Gross Income in cash to charities in 2020 and 2021 (old limit was 50% and 60% depending on the year).

2. **Retirement Plans**: The period for 401k and IRA exemption from the 10% penalty on withdrawals from these plans due to COVID was extended to 60 days after 12/27/2020 (2/25/2021 if my math is correct). This applies to up to $100,000 in withdrawals due to COVID and the rules allowing stretching taxes for three years or repaying within 3 years apply to these withdrawals. Basically, you can take money out, up to $100,000 due to needing it for COVID caused problems all the way out to late February of 2021, though you can't pull $100,000 in 2020 AND 2021. The $100,000 limit applies to ALL Coronavirus distributions.

3. **Disaster Losses**: The changes to deducting disaster losses above $500 due to COVID was also extended for 60 days after December 27th, 2020. This suspended the 10% of income rule that meant that a disaster had to be ENORMOUS before it made a difference on your taxes.

4. **Business Meal Deduction**: I have heard this one called the "3 Martini Lunch Rule". For 2021 and 2022, the 50% limit on meal deduction for businesses was raised to 100%. Simply put, a business owner can deduct 100% of business-related meals including those with clients.

5. **Education Credits**: The Tuition and Fees Deduction will be in effect for 2020, but not after. The Lifetime Learning Credit and

American Opportunity Credit will have their income limits matched (The LLC limit raised to equal the AOC limit) starting in 2021.

6. **Sick and Family Leave**: The qualifying period for employers to claim credits for paying employees while they are out sick or taking care of family due to COVID was extended to 3/31/2021. This applies to self-employed taxpayers who are out sick or shutdown and the law allows them to calculate based on 2019 or 2020 income whichever is better.

7. **Payroll Tax Holiday**: For those who took advantage of not having to pay Social Security Tax in the last quarter of 2020, the payback period has been extended for all of 2021, vice just the first few months. This means paybacks will be smaller, but last longer. This mostly applies to military and some Federal employees, though some civilian employers might have allowed opting in.

8. **Paycheck Protection Program**: More money was made available and eligible employers can come for more money if they meet certain requirements. The law was clarified to explicitly state that even if the loan is forgiven, expenses paid by loan proceeds remain deductible if allowed by current tax law.

9. **Earned Income Tax Credit (and child credits)**: You can use 2019 income vice 2020 income if it gets better results. This applies to EITC, Child Tax Credit and Additional Child Tax Credit. You use 2019 income for calculating all of them or none of them. You can't pick and choose.

10. **Educator Expense**: The $250 deduction for teachers paying for classroom supplies includes costs for protective equipment and other COVID related supplies such as masks or disinfectants.

11. **Flexible Spending Accounts**: Normally these accounts, which are usually used for childcare and health care, must be used before the end of the calendar year or the money is lost. Employers have several options for relief in this case, including allowing rollover of money to be used in 2021. Also, money for childcare normally has to

be used only for children under the age of 13. This age limit was raised to under 14 for 2021 only.

## Changes to Expiring Tax Provisions:

Mortgage Insurance Premiums remain deductible into 2021

Principle Residence Cancelled Debt Exclusion was extended through 2025, but the amount allowed to be excluded was reduced to $750,000 ($375,000 if MFS) starting in 2022.

The Non-Business Energy Efficient Credit was extended to 2021.

Exclusion of employer paid student loans of up to $5250 per year was extended through 2025.

The Solar Credit phaseout was modified and slightly extended. The percentage used for calculating the credit is 26% in 2021 and 2022, and 22% in 2023. The credit is not currently available for 2024 and later.

The increase in the percentage above which medical expenses were deductible was permanently changed back to 7.5%. It was supposed to go up to 10% with the passage of the Affordable Care Act but has been pushed of repeatedly and is now finally dead.

**The book continues with generic tax information, basic advice, and discussions of the previous tax laws passed in the Trump era, modified as necessary by the latest tax law changes:**

# Sunset Provisions and Zombie Rules

If there is one thing that we have learned since the passage of Trump Tax, it is that no tax law change is guaranteed to be permanent. The Mortgage Insurance Premium Deduction and Tuition and Fees Deduction are just two examples of provisions that just seem to come and go. Energy efficiency provisions appear and disappear, and the 10% limit on Medical Expense Deductions may NEVER go fully into effect (if you read the chapter previous to this one, you know this was a VERY accurate prediction of mine). Add to that the fact that many of these changes expire in 2025 and that means predictability is near to impossible. I have started labelling some of these items as "Zombie Rules" because you just cannot kill them – they won't stay dead.

I'm not going to talk about what provisions have sunsets and when they are set to expire (at least not in this edition) because we all know that Congress will change everything by then and, even if they don't, they won't just let them expire – too much political pressure.

This means that I may say something has been eliminated, even though it actually has been "suspended". I simply cannot be bothered to play the silly political games that were required to keep the Trump Tax Bill under $1.5 trillion dollars of cost.

I will try to identify Zombie Rules, so you know that even if I say they are dead, you realize they can reanimate at any time.

# Now Is a Good Time to Learn How Taxes Work

Everybody thinks they understand taxes, but very few people do. You do not have to become an expert, but you should understand the difference between a credit and a deduction. You should understand that what is taken out of your paycheck (or out of that retirement account you liquidated) is literally a GUESS as to how much taxes you owe. You file a tax RETURN to get a REFUND of excess taxes paid or to determine how much you still OWE. You should realize that going up a tax bracket is a GOOD thing (you make more money, but the higher tax rate is only applied to your income above the new bracket).

There is a lot of other stuff that you should get familiar with, including how your paycheck works with regard to taxes, the fact that FICA taxes aren't part of your tax return (they are gone until you collect Social Security or go on Medicare), and that the Internal Revenue Service isn't as evil and powerful as they are made out to be (though you still don't want to piss them off).

Take some time to begin to understand how all this works, and you will be better for it as your life goes on.

The next chapter is a good place to start on this.

# A Rundown of How Taxes Work

You probably know a lot of this intuitively, simply by having filed taxes before, but I want to review the basic tax process, so we have all the terms right when I discuss them later. In the age of software tax preparation, it is way too easy to let the program do magic without knowing what is happening behind the data entry, so this will help a bit.

You start with INCOME. For most people, this is their wages, which come from their W-2's. It also includes business, rental and investment, pension and retirement, unemployment and other miscellaneous income. In addition, alimony (before Trump Tax Changes), disability and Social Security income might be taxable. Add all that together and you get your TOTAL INCOME subject to tax.

Now we take some magic deductions, many of which have special rules or income limitations, such as student loan interest, moving expenses, some alimony paid, teacher expenses, traditional IRA contributions, a bit of charity, etc. and deduct these to get a very important number: ADJUSTED GROSS INCOME (AGI). These deductions are often called "above the line" deductions because they do not require you to itemize in order to subtract them. Knowing your AGI for a tax year can be very important, since most income limitations are based on it, and you often provide it as proof of identity when accessing your data or filing a tax return.

We are about to hit the part of taxes where FILING STATUS matters. See the next chapter if you are not certain what yours is.

Now we get to STANDARD or ITEMIZED DEDUCTION. To keep people from having to keep track of every little deductible expense, the IRS gives you a very large STANDARD DEDUCTION that you can take even if you do not actually have that much stuff to deduct. This is a good deal, and a major feature of the Trump Tax Change was to expand this number to reduce the amount of people required to itemize. For 2020, the STANDARD DEDUCTION is $12,400 for Single and Married Filing Separate Filers, $24,800 for Joint Filers and $18,650 for Head of Household Filers. If you add up your itemized deductions, made up primarily of state and local taxes paid, mortgage interest and charitable contributions, and it exceeds the STANDARD DEDUCTION, you take that bigger number and you have ITEMIZED your DEDUCTIONS.

Now you take your STANDARD or ITEMIZED DEDUCTIONS and subtract them from your AGI to get TAXABLE INCOME. It is exactly what it sounds like…this is what you pay taxes on.

Most people will look their TAXABLE INCOME up on a tax table to get the amount of taxes, but certain income is taxed at lower or higher rates, so you might need a worksheet…way too much info for here, but I need to take another aside and talk about Tax Brackets. As your income increases, you move up tax brackets. Most people think that when you enter the 22% tax bracket, all your TAXABLE INCOME gets taxed at 22%. That is not how it works. Here's how it really works, using rounded numbers for illustration only (not the actual tax bracket break points). For a Married Joint filer, the first $20,000 of income is taxed at 10%, $20,000 to $80,000 is taxed at 12% and ONLY the portion above $80,000 is taxed at 22% (unless the income enters one of the other 4 higher tax brackets) but the principle continues. Jumping a tax bracket is a GOOD thing!

So, after this calculation you have the amount of TAX.

At this point, we can lower the TAX by taking CREDITS. These reduce the tax amount dollar for dollar and are AWESOME! The most common is the $2,000 per child under 17 Child Tax Credit. There are also Education Credits, Child Care Credits, Saver's Credits and Foreign Tax Credits. These are also called non-refundable credits because they cannot reduce your tax due below zero.

Now we have ADDITIONAL TAXES. These are basically taxes that are not fully related to income taxes. The most common is self-employment tax, which business owners pay instead of Social Security and Medicare taxes. Take a look at your W-2 or pay stub. You see Federal Income Tax withheld, which is what a Federal tax return is all about, but you also see Social Security and Medicare taxes (also called FICA). Those taxes are GONE, and not even a discussion on your tax return. That said, the IRS is used to get those taxes from people who do not have an employer withhold them, or people who get the majority of their income from tips, such that there isn't enough paycheck to cover them. Other things you might see here are penalties for early retirement withdrawals and a bunch of Affordable Care Act (Obamacare) taxes.

Add these ADDITIONAL TAXES to your base TAX and you have TOTAL TAX. For most people, you compare your FEDERAL TAX WITHHELD from your pay to this number to get your REFUND or BALANCE DUE.

But wait! There are also REFUNDABLE CREDITS and ESTIMATED PAYMENTS. Estimated payments are basically exactly like withholding from a job, except that you sent it to the IRS directly, to make sure you did not owe. REFUNDABLE CREDITS are CREDITS that can get you back more money than you paid in. The most common are Earned Income Credit, Additional Child Tax Credit and the American Opportunity Credit (an Education Credit). Basically, they treat all these items just like the withholding from your paycheck to get your REFUND or BALANCE DUE.

One last thing, if you owe more than $1000, and do not meet an exception, you have to pay a PENALTY. You were supposed to have paid taxes on your income as you earned it, not after you filed your taxes. Poop…

# What is My Filing Status?

A quick note on some changes: There are a couple updates to this over the last two years. One is that during the Coronavirus pandemic they have suspended collecting back taxes and most everything else other than Child Support out of refunds and stimulus checks as discussed in the Married Filing Separately reasons. The other involves Head of Household, which has its own chapter way later in the book.

This is the first decision you need to make about filing your taxes, though for most people they do not have a lot of choice. This is sometimes the easiest question to answer, and sometimes the most complicated. I am going to try to put the facts you need down, in an order that will help you make the decision as easily as possible.

I'm going to start by getting the easy situations out of the way, so you can avoid a long chapter:
- If you are unmarried, have no children and live alone, you are probably going to file SINGLE.
- If you are married (as of 12/31 of the tax year) and live with your spouse, you are going to file MARRIED FILING JOINTLY (MFJ) or MARRIED FILING SEPARATELY (MFS).
- If you are a single parent of your own minor child and it is just you and your children in your home all year, you are probably going to file HEAD OF HOUSEHOLD (HH).

Here are the details:

1. There are five filing statuses available. They are SINGLE, MARRIED FILING JOINTLY (MFJ), MARRIED FILING SEPARATELY (MFS), HEAD OF HOUSEHOLD (HH) and QUALIFYING WIDOWER (QW). I'm going to use the abbreviations from now on.
2. If you are married and not legally separated on December 31st of the tax year, you are MARRIED. This means you have to file MFJ or MFS unless you meet very unique requirements to file HH by

being considered unmarried for tax purposes (covered next). Legal separation requires the involvement of the courts and is governed by the laws of your state.

3. If you are not divorced or legally separated, you can be considered unmarried if ALL the following apply:

     a. You did not live with your spouse after June 30th of the tax year. This does not count if it is a temporary absence, such as school or military orders. The idea is that the other parent left and is not coming back.

     b. You paid over half the costs of maintaining a home, which was the main home for your child, stepchild or foster child for at least 6 months and a day of the tax year. A foster child must be placed with you by an authorized placement agency or court. Note that the relations are VERY specific. One way to think of it is that you as a parent have been forced to take care of a child for whom you are responsible due to being the birth parent, step-parent or foster parent. I should also note that step-relationships established by marriage do not end by divorce or death.

     c. You claim that child on your tax return as a dependent, unless you could claim the child, but are allowing the child's other parent to claim them under special rules for divorced or separated parents.

4. The requirement of paying more than half the cost of maintaining a home discussed in this section are different from most tax situations involving support. In this case, it is just for the home. You include taxes, interest and rent paid (some tax situations will talk about Fair Rental Value—here it is rent PAID). You also include utilities, repairs and insurance for the home. Other than that, it is food consumed in the home, and not much else. You need to have paid more than half of that total during the period of time the child lived with you (at least 6 months and a day).

5. If you meet all the requirements in 3 above, you can choose to file HH. You can also file MFJ if the other spouse agrees. If you file HH, the other spouse must file MFS, unless they meet the requirements of paragraph 3 above with a different child.

6. If you are married as discussed in paragraph 2 and do not meet the requirements of paragraph 3 (or are simply happily married), you can file MFJ or MFS. Generally, MFJ is better, but you can figure out your taxes both ways and choose the one that gets better results.

This book is not about MFS, but I'll list a few reasons to consider that MIGHT make you want or have to file MFS:

a. You do not want to be responsible for your spouse's taxes. If you file MFJ, you have to sign the return saying that everything is true under penalty of perjury, and the IRS will hold you accountable for what is on the tax return, even if all you did was sign it. It is very difficult to get the IRS to accept that you are not responsible for a joint return you signed (though there are ways). By filing a separate tax return, you are taking responsibility only for the information on YOUR tax return.

b. You might have to go MFS if you cannot get your spouse to file jointly with you. You cannot make them. This happens sometimes because your spouse does not want to be responsible for YOUR tax return, or during divorces or separations.

c. Your spouse owes debts that will be collected out of their refund, such as back child support, student loans or taxes. If you file separately, they will not take it out of your refund if you were not responsible. There are ways to avoid this without filing MFS (called Injured Spouse), but you should get professional help in these cases.

d. There are certain tax situations that do work out better MFS. Mainly they involve big differences in income, and either medical expenses or job expenses. You will have to run the numbers both ways to be sure.

e. You are making student loan payments with an Income Based Repayment Plan. Filing MFS means the payments are calculated only based on YOUR income. MFJ they include both spouse's income and your payments will be higher (if your spouse has income).

7. If your spouse or child died during the year, you may consider them to have lived with you and/or been married to you through the end of the year. If your spouse died during the year, you will still file MFJ or MFS with them. However, if you get remarried during the same year, you have to file MFJ or MFS with your NEW spouse, and you will file your deceased spouse's tax return as MFS.

8. If you have never had any children, and are not married, your filing status is SINGLE.

9. If you are not married, you may be able to claim HH if you pay half the costs of maintaining a home for someone who lived with you for more than half of the year. I discussed paying half the costs

of maintaining a home in paragraph 4 above. The person has to meet very specific requirements:

a. They must be your parent, son, daughter, stepchild, foster child (foster child must be placed with you by an authorized placement agency or court), brother, sister, stepbrother or stepsister, or a direct descendent of one of them (meaning nieces, nephews, grandchild, etc.)

b. If they are your parent, they do not have to live with you, but you have to pay the costs discussed in paragraph 4 for the home they live in (can be a nursing home). You also have to meet the requirements for claiming them as a dependent on your tax return, and you have to claim them to qualify for HH.

c. If they are not your parent, they must meet the following requirements:

- They must have lived with you more than 6 months and a day,
- You must claim them as a dependent,
- They must be under 19, or between 19 and 23 if a full-time student for at least five months, or if older, permanently and totally disabled, and
- They must not have provided more than half of their own support.

d. If you do not claim them only because they are married, someone else can claim them and does, or you allow the other parent to claim them under rules for divorced or separated parents, you can still be HH.

10. If none of the requirements for MFJ, MFS and HH apply, you are Single, with one major exception, covered next under 11.

11. If you were married and your spouse died during the year, you still file MFJ for the tax year they died in (unless you remarry). After that, there are special rules that might apply for the next two years if you have dependent children. You must not have remarried, the dependent must be your child or stepchild (not foster child), they must have lived with you ALL year, you must claim them as a dependent, you must have paid over half the cost of maintaining the home (discussed in paragraph 4) and you must have filed a MFJ return with the spouse in the year they died. If all those requirements are met, you file as QW, which basically gives you a lot of the

benefits of being married, even though you technically are not. After these two years of QW you would generally end up as HH as long as you continued to meet those requirements.

12. When discussing living with you in the above discussions, temporary absences for school, work, military, etc. still count as living with you.

**My Advice:**

1. If you get married, plan on filing jointly if at all possible. Run a rough estimate of your taxes shortly after getting married and make withholding adjustments as necessary.

2. Do NOT change withholding allowances to Married just because you got married. Use the new W-4 form (covered in a later chapter) to ensure you accurately account for BOTH of your incomes.

3. The IRS is looking hard at Head of Household. Make sure that you meet the requirements for using that filing status AND be sure that you can access paperwork to PROVE that you meet the requirements, especially relationship and living status information. This paperwork can be birth certificates, divorce records, adoption papers, school and doctor records. I cover this in more detail in a later chapter.

# The BIG HUGE Tax Advice Chapter

This is just a bunch of things everyone should know or do, all in one place. Feel free to skim…but make sure you follow the advice. A lot of this chapter is adapted from my other books, so if you are a fan of my stuff, it might look familiar. I include this stuff in most of my books in one form or another because the advice is just that damn important and useful.

## Unemployment Income is Taxable:

I added this at the very front of this chapter since a TON of people are receiving unemployment income and very few people realize it is taxable at the Federal level and very often by the state as well. Also, the default withholding amount of 10% for Federal is often insufficient to cover the amount of taxes due on the income. Bottom line: If you receive unemployment payments, it will usually reduce your refund or increase your balance due. This means that just as you might be getting back on your feet, you file a tax return and figure out that you're screwed. Advising someone trying to scrape by on unemployment to increase their withholding or set some money aside is a tough sell, but you need to be aware of this and take it into account, so you don't end up in a worse situation than you already are.

## Download a Copy of the Federal and State Instruction Books:

They are free. Put them on the back of the toilet and read them while you poop.

This is a great way to get familiar with what things you pay taxes on and what you can deduct. Walking through the instructions while looking at the forms gives you an idea how your taxes should be prepared, how the numbers on your W-2 translate into a tax amount, and give you an idea what your software should be spitting out – NEVER assume your software is outputting accurate results until you have looked at the forms, and ensured everything is in its proper place!

You would be amazed at what you find in those publications that might apply to you that your software forgets to mention. Remember, easy is not accurate, and software tries very hard to be easy. You might even find some deductions your tax guy missed! If you do, your tax guy should give you your money back and do the amendment for free - I would.

Have the books handy if you use software to file your taxes (or download a fresh copy if you're a germaphobe). These books also make quite powerful sleep aids - and they are definitely NOT habit forming.

## Always Print a Copy of Your Tax Returns

What a stupid piece of advice! I mean, seriously, isn't this obvious?

Based on how often I am asked to get someone a copy of their tax return in the middle of summer, no it is not. Print a copy, put it with all the supporting documents, and throw it in a safe place. I like one of those small, top opening file boxes. I keep stuffing the returns in until the new one doesn't fit, then I shred the oldest one. You should have 4 years at a minimum, but I probably have 7 to 10 years in mine.

You may need your 2019 tax return to get the most out of your 2020 taxes due to a recent rule allowing to use 2019 income to calculate 2020 Earned Income Tax Credit.

While you're at it, if you can get an electronic copy, save that on your computer, and your backup hard drive, and maybe even a floppy disk (ask your Dad if you don't know what that is). When you move, these files go with YOU, not in the moving van.

Let me add that, a little time spent anywhere that people ask tax questions (God help me, Reddit is a cesspool of tax ignorance), will enlighten you that needing information from a prior year tax return is the absolute most common tax topic. You cannot even e-file your current tax return without knowing your prior year Adjusted Gross

Income (AGI). Most people don't know this because their software remembers it for them and/or a professional does not need it.

Need to file FASFA or buy a house – you're gonna need that tax return. And that letter from the IRS…good luck if you can't find the tax return.

## Update Your Address with the IRS and Your State

I know these first bits of advice are starting to make it seem like this book is filled with a bunch of really obvious stuff, but these bits of advice are based on REAL LIFE. The vast majority of tax problems we deal with would be significantly less of a problem, and be much easier to deal with if people printed a copy of their tax return and updated their address with the IRS:

EVERY TIME YOU MOVE!

Believe it or not, the IRS does not automatically know that you have moved, and the U.S. Postal Service is not competent enough to trust that a Change of Address form will work. The IRS sends letters to the address on your tax return if you haven't changed it using the proper form. If the letter suggests a change to your tax return, the clock starts ticking on disputing it as soon as they send it. Updating the IRS when you move will save you a TON of heartache. This happens way too often and is way too easy to prevent.

Here is an IRS site with more information:

https://www.irs.gov/taxtopics/tc157.html

You're on your own for the state, but their Revenue Department website should make it easy.

I can tell you now that the stimulus check fun we are currently experiencing is made worse for the people who did not follow this advice.

If you are going to college, joining the military or moving around a lot, you might want to use your parent's address until you are settled.

## Do not Fear the IRS

If you aren't cheating, you have very little to worry about beyond money and hassle. Obviously, these are not trivial things, but very few people go to jail over taxes. Some tax people like to scare you with the IRS, and, if you are cheating, you should be scared. I prefer to scare people with the prospect of not getting all they deserve.

How about we use an example: Say you've got a nice sofa to donate to charity. You check some stores and eBay, and the values are between $500 and $1000 dollars. Assuming the $1000 is not a huge outlier, take the $1000. It is reasonable, defensible, and not frivolous. If you are in the 22% tax bracket, that's $110 on your tax return, plus some from the State! Now let's say the mean old IRS does its worst, and face to face audits you. The auditor looks at your documents and tells you the sofa is only worth $500. You argue a bit, but he insists, and you have to pay back the $110, plus a bit of interest. No handcuffs, no jail-time, no yelling or beatings. You shake hands, sign some paperwork and write a check. Now let us pretend we're in Vegas. You find a table that gives you $110, and then you spin a wheel, and if you lose you have to give them the $110 back, plus $15, except you only lose 1 out of 100 times! Who would not make that bet? That's the same thing we're talking about with the desk.

JUST DON'T CHEAT!

## Do not Lie to the IRS

Don't ignore them either.

Exaggerate, stretch, manipulate, but DO NOT LIE. Two things the IRS hates more than anything: being lied to and being ignored. They are like your parents. I encourage taking the most aggressive tax position you can that is not a lie or frivolous.

Do be aware that if you get aggressive, you need to be prepared to lose in a fight with the IRS. Know how much money you are risking by being aggressive and be prepared to pay some or all of it back at a later date. Odds are you will get to keep the money, but it's good to be prepared.

## Don't Do Things Just for the Tax Benefit

There are very few things that will improve your taxes without costing you in other areas of your life. You only get a portion of any deduction off your taxes, so often times not paying something is better than getting the deduction.

People who tell you not to pay off your home mortgage because it is your best tax deduction are just stupid. You pay $10,000 in interest to get $2200 back on your taxes (22% tax bracket). BRILLIANT! You're out $7800. Of course, the tax benefit combined with other realities (like you don't have $200,000 to pay the mortgage off or you have better things to do with the money – economists call this opportunity cost) can make this a smart idea, but don't just do it for the taxes.

As a point of fact, most things that are good for your taxes, you actually do for better, non-tax reasons:

Health Savings Account? For your health.
401k or IRA? For your future.
Kids? Seriously, if you're having kids for the tax benefits, you are doing it wrong. VERY WRONG.

## The Income Tax is Not Illegal

I am not kidding.

All those people screaming about not filing taxes and getting away with it are full of dookie (though they may get away with it for a while because the IRS sucks at enforcement).

There are tons of examples of BS arguments: the 16th amendment was never properly ratified, taxes are voluntary, filing zero returns, wages aren't income...all CRAP.

The IRS will not only dismiss your attempt to argue this muck but can actually fine you MORE (a lot more – up to $25,000) just for trying. They can also fine your tax guy or lawyer for arguing these things.

These situations have been thoroughly litigated, many all the way to the Supreme Court. The income tax is SETTLED LAW.  Do not fall for these things. I don't like taxes and would give up my entire career if they did away with the income tax, but living a fantasy where the entire government is wrong and everybody is just living in ignorance and that there is some simple, easy way to avoid taxes is just plain fantasy.

The 7th Circuit Court of Appeals put it best: "Like moths to a flame, some people find themselves irresistibly drawn to the tax protester movement's illusory claim that there is no legal requirement to pay federal income tax. And, like moths, these people sometimes get burned." United States v. Sloan (7th Circuit 1991).

## The IRS Didn't Call You

Unless you are currently involved in communications with the IRS that were initiated by you in person or by the IRS via a letter, that person calling claiming to be the "IRS" is full of you know what.

The IRS does NOT initiate communications via phone calls. Scammers trying to steal your money or identity do.

I have already had TONS of people (including me) receive these kinds of calls. These guys are professionals, and they can often sound very convincing, and will even threaten to arrest you. Swear at them and hang up.

Lately they have gotten more sophisticated and are even sending relatively real-looking letters. Always assume someone calling and asking for money or personal information is a scam – tax based or not. Independently look the agency's contact information up online and call direct.

If they ask you to pay with gift cards…it is a scam. Seriously, how do people think the IRS wants iTunes gift cards?

As far as the Coronavirus stimulus checks, the ONLY way the IRS will communicate with you on this is the letter they are required to send within 15 days of sending you the money. Any email, phone call or text is a scam! The only way you can update your direct deposit information is on the IRS "Get My Payment" app or calling 1 (800) 919-9835.

## Pay Attention to Your Withholding

You should check every pay stub, every time, and make sure your withholding is consistent. It is also a good way of ensuring you get paid what you earned.

The amount coming out of your paycheck for taxes should stay the same if your pay stays the same, go up if your pay goes up, and go down if your pay goes down (obvious, I know). If you want to be extra careful, you can track your year to date withholding numbers and make sure it lines up with the prior year.

Payroll people sometimes make mistakes, so you need to keep an eye on this, and find out why if things change drastically. Do not just assume that everything is fine. Tax time is a bad time to find out something was wrong. The IRS will not let you use a payroll error as an excuse to avoid taxes. It is YOUR responsibility to ensure enough is taken from your check.

The IRS has a new Tax Withholding Estimator that can be very useful for checking where you are on withholding. If you are careful with it and use your paystubs, you can get a very good feel for your refund amount as well as get advice on correcting it with a revised W-4. More on this later.

A couple years ago, I discovered halfway through tax season that my employer was not withholding ANY state taxes. I had to have them withhold ONE THOUSAND DOLLARS every two weeks for the rest of the season to make up the difference.

## Tax Software Sucks

Tax software has to be both user friendly, easy to use, and accurate. If it is not user friendly and easy to use, no one is going to pay for it. Hell, that's why it's so popular! It is simply NOT possible to cover all the complexities of tax law and still be easy to use. So, they make it easy to use: "How much did you pay for uniforms?" Sure, there is probably an info button you can click that will go into all the nitty gritty of this question, but if you read them every time they come up, it's not simple and easy anymore. "How many miles did you drive for business last year?" Again, many pop-ups will be available to help you navigate the dizzying rules that are involved in this simple question, but you're not likely to read them, and, if you do, they're only going to make you more confused. Don't even get me started on depreciation, business use of home, or investing income!

And that's just the Federal return!

Many states have nearly incomprehensible tax laws, and dozens of deductions and credits that you pretty much need to know exist in order to take advantage of them. Most software just drags things from the Federal to the State, with barely a peep about what deductions you might miss. I cannot even begin to describe the messes I have seen from tax software. Recently, a client who had only one W-2, no wife, no kids, no house, and an amazingly simple Federal 1040EZ missed out on over $10,000 in state tax money over the previous dozen years because either the software didn't ask, or he neglected to answer enough questions to establish that his military income was exempt from California taxes. Most of that money is gone forever.

Tax preparation software SUCKS! You will have a better chance at an accurate return using pen and paper with the Federal and State instructions than you will using software!

## There is No "Table"

So, you cannot be paid "Under" it.

As a general rule, every dollar you make, especially if it is for providing goods or services, is taxable. Just because you get paid in cash and there is no paperwork does not change this.

I'm not your Mother or conscience, so I can't make you do something you don't want to, but I can tell you that the law is very clear on this, and if you decide not to declare income, the penalties can be very harsh. There is also generally no statute of limitations on hiding income from the IRS.

I have seen, many times, where someone thinks they are being paid "under the table" when in reality their employer was paying them as a contractor and reporting the money to the IRS. Several years later, massive tax bills start arriving. You see, if someone pays you to help their business, they cannot deduct it on THEIR taxes unless they report it to the IRS. So, they may imply it's under the table, but paying you as a contractor is simple and easy for them to do, and they will often do it, sometimes without giving you the copy you need to file taxes. Also, contractors pay an extra 15% (roughly) in taxes, and there is no withholding to cover ANY of it!

Beware of "The Table"!

To satisfy technicality nags, if you are paid under $600, the person who paid you does not have to report it to the IRS, but you still have to claim it as income. Also, contractors pay taxes on their "net" income, not their "gross" income, but that is not the point of this advice.

## Tax Pros are NOT All the Same

You can be a paid tax preparer. Right now. All you need is a Tax Professional ID Number and you can get that online in 5 minutes for less than $100. No training, no test, nothing.  Don't believe me? Ask the IRS:

https://www.irs.gov/tax-professionals/understanding-tax-return-preparer-credentials-and-qualifications

Your tax guy may not even be able to represent you at an audit!

I personally think you need an Enrolled Agent or a CPA to prepare your taxes (if they have EA after their name, like, say, Kirk Taylor, EA, then they are an Enrolled Agent – or a liar). If you use a CPA, make sure they specialize in taxes like yours. CPA's know a lot more than Enrolled Agents, just not necessarily about taxes. EA's are tax specialists; CPA's have a much broader knowledge base.

Pick your preparer wisely – get referrals. If you don't like what's happening at the desk, don't like the results, or don't like the fees, take your papers and walk out. If the preparer isn't okay with this, and still wants you to pay, then you made the right choice by leaving.

Good preparers don't expect to be paid unless the client is 100% satisfied (within reason of course – I can't magic away your balance due when you or your employer messed up your withholding).

The link above has access to the IRS list of credentialled preparers who are in good standing, though it in no way guarantees that they are a great preparer. It is still a good place to start.

If you get Earned Income Tax Credit and your tax pro doesn't ask for your 2019 tax return numbers – run away! Unless of course they prepared your 2019 taxes.

## The Tax Prep Guarantee You Get Is NOT What You Think It Is

Unless you pay your Tax Dude extra, specifically for an extended guarantee, he or she probably is not providing you the kind of guarantee you probably think you deserve. Most guarantees cover interest and penalties, not taxes. This makes sense since you would have owed the taxes anyway if the idiot hadn't messed them up. So, by the preparer paying the interest and penalties, you get an interest free loan from Uncle Sam.

This is, of course, little consolation when you have to come up with three grand to pay your Uncle Sam back because your Tax Genius turns out to be a Tax Dunce. I personally would only have taxes done by a SUPER Tax Genius (see my blog).

They may also charge you for help in responding to the IRS, especially if you get a face to face audit. This is actually quite fair since the time and effort can be extensive. Additionally, many will try to claim that you didn't provide them the right information and documents (and they will often be right).

Oh, and that guarantee you get with your software – it's not worth squat. It is very easy for them to claim that YOU just did not put the right information in or didn't follow the instructions correctly. As best I can tell from my experiences, it basically only covers if the programmer's messed up.

### Get a Professional Tax Review Once in a While

Tax software sucks. It really does.
I know I sound like a broken record on this.

That does not mean you have to pay for a review. Many professional preparers will check your return for free, and then quote you a non-obligatory price for them to fix it. This is a win-win. Do it every four years at least (this ensures that it is not too late to get your money back).

You get peace of mind, and maybe some money.

This does not just apply to software. If you have been using the same tax pro for years, without really paying attention to the results, you might be getting screwed. Give a new guy (or gal) a chance to see what they can do.

This, of course, does not apply to me – I am perfect – akin to the Tax Unicorn.

## If Your Tax Pro Tells You to Do Something...Do It

It should not make me as happy as it does when my clients take my advice, but it does.

I spend a lot of time coming up with brilliant ideas (hence this book) and great advice, yet a noticeable minority of my clients ignore my wonderful advice. This is often to their severe detriment. Obviously, there are levels to this, but when your tax pro gets really serious, leans over the table, looks you in the eyes and gestures emphatically, it's time to pay attention. If they write something down – do it! One of my greatest skills as a tax pro is not cursing under my breath when I see that my important suggestions were blown off. This accomplishment is just below this year's goal of not asking, "What year?" when getting the birthdate of a newborn child.

## Call Your Tax Guy When...

You have debt getting cancelled.
You want to take money out of a retirement account.
You want to change your withholding (other than minor tweaks).
You are going to work overseas.
Someone tells you to do something for the tax benefit.
You are selling your rental property.
You are moving money around in investment accounts.
You are retiring.
Your income will go up a lot.
You are starting a new job.
You are starting a business.
You start collecting unemployment.
You are going to be paid on a 1099MISC.

Anything else that might change your tax situation, or you have any questions at all. People do not call (or email) their tax person often enough. That is what you pay for. If you use software...email a tax guy you trust. Some of these aren't absolutes, like moving money around investment accounts at the same level you do every year.

Let me add that for non-time sensitive questions, e-mail is the preferred communication method. It allows the professional to take the time to look up your tax information, research the question and form a clear and easy to follow response that you can refer back to if needed, rather than remembering what they told you. If your preparer does not efficiently respond to emails (72 hours) find a new one.

## Don't Call the IRS Unless...

The IRS is under-staffed and over busy. I don't have a lot of sympathy for them, but I do have sympathy for people who really need to talk to them and can't get through. This means I hate it when people call them for stupid crap that could be handled online or other ways. Here is a list of when NOT to call them:

1. Your refund is delayed unless it has been AT LEAST 21 days AND you checked "Where's My Refund" at irs.gov and followed any instructions there.
2. Your tax return has been rejected. If you cannot solve it without calling the IRS – mail your return in.
3. You have a non-time sensitive question and it is between January and April.
4. You have a generic tax question. Look it up or call a tax pro – the IRS will give you the wrong answer anyway. I'm not kidding, and you can still get in trouble for listening to them.
5. You need last year's AGI or a copy of a tax return or a transcript. Sign up to get them online.
6. You have not gotten your stimulus check. I really mean this. It won't help.

Call the IRS if:

1. The IRS tells you to.
2. The "Where's My Refund" site at irs.gov tells you to.
3. You have a letter with a specific number to call.

4. Your tax pro tells you to.

## Tax Resolution Companies Are Often Rip-offs

You know the ones I'm talking about. The ones advertised on TV or radio that say they can reduce your back taxes by thousands, get the IRS off your back, stop the garnishments, etc. I'm sure some might be good, legitimate companies, but most are little more than one trick ponies.

They will file an Offer in Compromise (OIC), which will stop the liens and levies (as they promised). Unfortunately, the IRS does not approve many of these so, when they say no, the problem comes back full force, and you're out a bunch of money you paid to the tax resolution company. If you owe back taxes, talk to a local professional with good references.

More on Offers in Compromise: As a general rule, an Offer requires doubt as to whether you owe the taxes assessed, or a doubt that you will EVER have the ability to pay it back. This is a long, slow, uphill battle with a high likelihood of failure. And the resolution company will make you do almost all of the work.

## There is a Tax Hit for Canceled Debt

We are talking about mortgages, student loans, credit cards, cars or any other debt. Getting debt cancelled is a total win and a happy dance is called for. Until the 1099C comes, which sometimes does not happen for a while, or at all - but the IRS gets it. Then a CP2000 letter appears saying you owe money on the canceled debt as if it were income.

Bummer.

The point is, if you get debt canceled, including student loans, car repossessions and foreclosures, be prepared for the 1099C, and the tax hit.

There are ways to avoid paying taxes on canceled debt, and not all student loan cancelations are taxable. The main exceptions are insolvency and if it was your principal residence, but these are complex, and you should seek professional help on them BEFORE tax time.

## Pay Your Child Support, Student Loans and Taxes

The IRS can and will take your tax refund to pay these things and more. It is called an offset, and there is very little you can do about it. If it's your spouse's debt you can try filing an injured spouse claim to get your portion of the refund.

They won't do it on your first missed payment, but when these things go into default, they will come get it and there is very little that you can do about it, other than the injured spouse thing.

Other unpaid things that will cause this are: military bonuses or pay that has to be paid back, social security or disability payments that have to be paid back, military exchange credit cards that aren't paid, and even unpaid State taxes. There are a lot of things they CAN use this for, but don't, so the list can change any day.

You can call 1-800-304-3107 to see if they are coming after your refund, though be aware that debts can be added between the time you call and getting your refund. The number covers everything EXCEPT owing the IRS for Federal taxes.

States are getting in on this act and collecting medical bills, property taxes, utility bills and all manner of other debts. One big sign that the reduced refund you got was due to debt is if the refund is not an even dollar amount.

During the Coronavirus pandemic, the Treasury Department has suspended the offset program for both tax refunds and stimulus payments. The exception to this is Back Child Support. This does not mean that you don't still owe the money, nor does it mean that interest and penalties are not continuing to accrue.

## Watch Out For a 1099MISC Job

Most people are employees. They get paid on a W-2, and their employer handles Social Security, Medicare and Income Tax Withholding. Your employer also matches your Social Security and Medicare taxes out of their own pocket. This is 7.65% of your income.

Because of this matching, your employer would rather you be an independent contractor paid on a 1099MISC. This makes all taxes YOUR responsibility. A lot of times, this is the right way to do things, like for real estate agents and a lot of construction workers. Sometimes it's shaky, and sometimes it's horsepucky.

You should find out, as soon as you take a job, how you are going to get paid, especially if you're in construction. If you're going to be on a 1099MISC, you should probably talk to a professional immediately to make sure you do everything the right way.

If you think you should be on a W-2, but they put you on a 1099MISC, talk to a tax professional about filing Form SS-8 and other forms to avoid paying both halves of Social Security and Medicare.

When you get paid by ANYBODY, you should confirm how they will report it to the IRS and what they are going to withhold. If they are paying you on a 1099MISC and not withholding, set side about 30% for taxes. This is probably overkill, but it's better than a big balance due later.

## Pay Attention to State Taxes

Your tax software is probably not nearly as good at doing State taxes as it is at doing Federal taxes (and it is not that good at Federal anyway). Your tax guru might not be that good at the states that he does not live in either.

It can be very worthwhile to spend some time researching tax deductions and credits for your state and reading the instruction booklet when doing your taxes. Also, if you have a state tax return done by a professional that is not working in that state, ask him about his knowledge of the state, and check things carefully. Tax pros are prickly about being questioned, and we hate admitting we don't know everything, but state taxes are one place where you need to call us on our arrogance.

In addition, if you work in a state, even if you are not a resident, you probably owe them taxes. Employers can really suck at accounting for this on your W-2. Normally if you live and work in different states, the state you live in taxes everything, the state you work in taxes the income earned in their state, and the state you live in gives you a credit for the taxes you paid to the other state so you're not double taxed. Some states have agreements with their bordering states that modify this. These are called reciprocal agreements and you probably need expert help with them because they are a bunch of legalese voodoo.

## Get Organized!

Organization is the core of success in everything you do. Taxes, College, Jobs, Life...it all hinges on knowing where your stuff is.

I know, you think you just aren't good at it. Hogwash. Organization is a skill just like everything else. It requires you to work at it, learn about it and practice it. Find out what works for you and do it!

This doesn't mean your desk and everything around it has to be perfectly organized and neat, but you should be able to find important notes and paperwork without too much trouble.

You need to write down expenses for tax information in a single, easy to find place.

You need a single to-do list that is with you wherever you go.

You need a calendar where you write down important events and due dates.

If you're an app person – use an app. If you're a software person – use software. Phone person – use your phone. Paper person – use a notebook. Organizer person – use an organizer. Whatever works for you.

The only thing that does not work is continuing to be disorganized and losing or forgetting important things.

**Have an Emergency Fund**

This is probably the best piece of advice that nobody follows. Having some cash tucked away makes a broken-down car, emergency travel, job loss or other unexpected expenses a problem, but not a catastrophe. A good tax refund is a nice way to start one.

Your emergency fund should be 3 to 6 months of living expenses.

The cool thing about having an emergency fund, is that this dude named Murphy, who has a law named after him, keeps track of who does and who does not have an emergency fund. Emergencies happen to people without an emergency fund, and generally do not happen to people who are prepared to handle them.

You should also have a budget, preferably one that has a budget item that puts money into your emergency fund at a rate that would refill it in 36 months or less. If it gets overfunded you can shift the money to something fun, but budgets keep your money under control, help avoid excess debt accumulation and let you plan for the future.

While I was writing this book, the Coronavirus Pandemic was at full swing, and millions of people had lost their jobs. Having an emergency fund would help a lot of those people. This is not meant as an I told you so for those who are suffering, but just advice for the future.

**Start Saving Now**

This is less about a specific plan or goal, and more about developing a habit. Being able to save will help you in a myriad of ways in your future. Start by saving for small goals, like your next TV or a newer car. Then build up to saving for retirement, a house, vacations, new cars etc. Everything that you might use a credit card to buy is something you should save for instead. It takes longer to get some things, but you end up paying a lot less for them.

These are the things I have a savings fund for:

Long Term Emergency Fund (new roof type thing)
Short Term Emergency Fund (broken appliance type thing)
Vacation
Car Repairs
New Car
VIP tickets to an annual celebrity golf tournament
Vacation Home Annual Fees (NOT a timeshare – a family home)
Christmas and Birthday Gifts
Vacation Home Addition

I used to have a fund for retirement, but it is now fully funded – and I am already semi-retired. I also used to have a lot of categories for furniture, remodels and other things, but I overfund my emergency fund so much that they generally end up having extra money in them for those things. I do not save for a house because mine is paid for now.

You can set up your savings based on your life and what you expect to need. Mine are obviously different than a lot of peoples because of the stage in life I am in and my weird career situation.

**Invest in Tax Sheltered Accounts**

There are very few sure-fire ways to save money on taxes. This is one of them. I'm talking about 401k's, IRA's, 457's, SIMPLE's, 403b's, SEP's, TSP's and all the other fancy account types out there. Many of them can be done right through your job and come right out of your paycheck. I will let your financial guy (NOT a banker) help you navigate which one and why, but all of them save you money on taxes, either now or in the future. Put as much in them as you can afford. The only specific advice I will give is that if your employer has a match to your contributions, invest enough to get the match before you do any other investing. Free money beats everything.

As a general rule, the younger you are, the more you should focus on Roth type accounts, but you really should talk to a financial advisor and not just your tax person.

When I said earlier not to do something just for the tax benefit, this is the time to ignore that advice. Talk to your financial advisor AND your tax dude to figure out the right TYPE of retirement account to invest in, and what investments to focus on – but invest in them for sure!

Every time you get a raise, your investments get a raise! This is most easily accomplished by bumping your 401k, or similar account percentage up when you get a raise, such that your paycheck still increases, but so does your savings rate.

**Maximize Health Savings Account Benefits (DON'T SKIP THIS PART)**

Health Savings Accounts are one of the best places to have your money stashed. It combines all the tax benefits of Roth AND Traditional retirement accounts. This means that the obvious way to use these accounts is not the most effective. Since these accounts can carry into retirement, and you will have medical expenses in retirement, investing in these accounts and letting them grow is VERY good for your future.

So, here is my basic advice:

1. Maximize your investment into HSA's, in coordination with your other retirement accounts, with the goal of maxxing out your allowed contribution.
2. Try not to use money out of the accounts except for truly unaffordable expenses. For sure don't use the money for every little copay or prescription.

3. Once you have around 150% of the maximum annual out of pocket deductible in the account, start investing it in the same manner as your 401k or IRA.

4. In retirement, pull money out of the HSA to match your medical expenses for a given year. You do not have to use the money in an HSA directly for the expense, you just have to have the expense. Your Medicare premiums taken from your Social Security can be used to justify pulling that amount from your HSA. None of this money will be taxed.

## Make More Money

I am closing with this to make a point. People ask me all the time how to pay less in taxes. The goal is obviously to have more money after taxes. The problem is that it can be a lot easier, with the same investment in time and effort, to make more money than to save in taxes.

Do not get tunnel vision on the taxes you pay. If you can make more money, forcing you to pay more in taxes, you will almost always come out ahead.

This also means that spending money because it is "deductible" can be one of the dumbest things to do.

# What Has NOT Changed in the Last Few Years

Now we can get to the tax law changes. I feel like it is a good start to talk about what has not changed. This with the understanding that a lot changes a little every year, but we are talking about what Congress left alone.

There was a lot of talk and a lot of bills passed. Below is a partial list of things that were talked about or worried about, that have not significantly changed:

Capital Gains tax rates stayed mostly the same, but the points at which they increased were decoupled from tax brackets, though the numbers are still pretty close.

Identification of sold securities unchanged (no forced FIFO) *

No change to the American Opportunity Credit or Lifetime Learning Credit, other than income limits merging for 2021 and later. The Tuition and Fees Deduction keeps disappearing and reappearing, then disappearing again and then coming back retroactively like some sort of zombie.

Student loan interest is still deductible.

Savings bond interest used for education is still tax free.

Colleges can still provide tax free education to their employees.

Electric vehicle credit was not changed, but vehicles continue to phase out as more of them are sold.

Employer education expense exclusion is unchanged.

No change to MSA deductibility.

No change to educator expense deduction other than clarifying that COVID related expenses count**

No change to the sale of personal residence exclusion***

No change to Dependent Care Benefits exclusion except for some temporary changes due to COVID.

No major change to adoption rules.

No change to the solar credit, except to slightly change the phaseout It drops from a 30% credit in 2019 and before, to a 26% credit in 2020/2021/2022, a 22% credit in 2023 and none thereafter. I seriously expect this to be a zombie credit that keeps getting revived at various times for various amounts.

No change to the Credit for Elderly and Disabled.

No change to Earned Income Credit other than normal annual inflation adjustments and a one year option to use 2019 income to calculate 2020 EITC.

No change to employer provided housing rules.

No change to exempt organizations rules on "politicking"

529 plans still cannot be used for homeschooling expenses

*There was a proposal to force partial sales of batches of stocks or other assets to be determined based on "First In, First Out" rules, rather than allowing the person selling to specify what shares of stock among a batch were the ones sold. This was not adopted.

**As will be discussed later, a whole bunch of itemized deductions were eliminated including the employee business expense deduction that teachers often use to deduct expenses above the $250 educator expense deduction.

***I am actually going to briefly cover the rules in a later chapter since people still think they have to buy a new home to make this work – something that was changed over 20 years ago.

# The Long Sordid Tax Forms Tale

NOTE: None of this should be construed as a political statement for or against a specific political party, though there is a bit of fun made at general government and politician incompetence.

Back before Trump Tax, there were three main tax forms. The 1040 Long Form, the 1040A Short Form and the 1040EZ. Most people could get away with the 1040A, and only people with very simple tax lives could use the 1040EZ. Everyone could use the 1040, but it was LOOOONG.

Congress in the Obama years decided that seniors needed their own EZ tax form, so they mandated that the IRS develop the 1040SR form. The mandate for this form was that it be as easy to use as the 1040EZ, but still allow all the things most seniors had: Social Security income, retirement income on 1099R Forms, investment income from 1099 forms, etc. These instructions were, of course, completely contradictory, so they gave the IRS a bunch of money, and a few years to get it done, so they were diligently working on it when Trump came into office.

The Trump tax reform envisioned one, super easy tax form for everyone, so they simplified the 1040 (mainly by moving everything off the 1040 onto schedules) such that the 1040 was basically a half sheet of paper, front and back, like a postcard. Not that anyone printed it as a half sheet front and back, but it was important to call it a postcard. This allowed the elimination of the 1040A and 1040EZ, so for 2018 taxes we had one tax form, and 6 schedules.

But nobody remembered to eliminate the 1040SR, or they still wanted it, so in 2019, the 1040SR was revealed. It looked suspiciously like the regular 1040, with two main differences: it included a table of standard deductions right on the form, and the font was bigger. In my system, the bigger font was easy to miss, but when I saw the pre-printed forms from the IRS, the print was HUGE!

They also eliminated 3 of the schedules in 2019, so for 2019 tax year we had a 1040, 1040SR and 3 schedules. The two forms were pretty much interchangeable, and, best as I can tell, home software and professional preparers are not distinguishing between the two when it comes to fees. It just happens that if you meet the requirements for the 1040SR, your printed return has a standard deduction table on it, and bigger print.

What about 2020 tax year? Well, considering the fact that Congress is passing tax bills left and right, including a stimulus that will need reconciling with 2020 tax returns, I am guessing at least one more schedule is coming. But who the heck knows?

# The New Tax Rates

The Trump Tax Law made most tax rates better for almost everyone. Generally speaking, a given amount of taxable income (after all deductions, but before credits) had a lower amount of tax on it. There was a lot of talk of simplification, but we had 7 tax brackets before the new law passed, and we still have 7. Before they were 10 percent, 15, 25, 28, 33, 35 and 39.6. Now they are 10 percent, 12, 22, 24, 32, 35 and 37. The points at which you moved brackets changed as well. Exact 2020 numbers are below.

Now, to revisit a common misconception, when you cross into a bracket, you do not suddenly pay that rate on all your income, just the amount in the new bracket. As an example, a Single person, under the new rates (using 2020 tax rates for this example), will ALWAYS pay 10 percent on their taxable income up to $9,875, and then 12 percent above that, up to the next bracket at $40,125. Only the portion of their taxable income above $40,125 gets taxed at 22% (up to the start of the next bracket.)

Here are the 2020 Tax Rates:

| Rate | Single | Married Filing Jointly (QW) |
|------|--------|------------------------------|
| 10% | Up to $9,875 | Up to $19,750 |
| 12% | $9,876 to $40,125 | $19,751 to $80,250 |
| 22% | $40,126 to $85,525 | $80,251 to $171,050 |
| 24% | $85,526 to $163,300 | $171,051 to $326,600 |
| 32% | $163,301 to $207,350 | $326,601 to $414,700 |
| 35% | $207,351 to $518,400 | $414,701 to $622,050 |
| 37% | Over $518,400 | Over $622,050 |

| Rate | Married Separately | Head of Household |
|------|--------------------|--------------------|
| 10% | Up to $9,875 | Up to $14,100 |
| 12% | $9,876 to $40,125 | $14,101 to $53,700 |
| 22% | $40,126 to $85,525 | $53,701 to $85,500 |
| 24% | $85,526 to $163,300 | $85,501 to $163,300 |
| 32% | $163,301 to $207,350 | $163,301 to $207,350 |
| 35% | $207,351 to $311,025 | $207,351 to $518,400 |
| 37% | Over $311,025 | Over $518,400 |

A couple things of note (but most people don't care about) are that Single and Married Filing Separate brackets are pretty much identical except at the point you hit the highest bracket, and a similar thing happens with Single and Married Filing Jointly, such that there is no marriage penalty except where you hit the highest bracket (the rest of the Joint table is double the Single table). Head of Household is only advantageous below the 22% bracket, and then basically mirrors the Single bracket. This advantage at lower incomes is one of the big plusses of filing Head of Household, along with increased income limits for a lot of credits.

**My Advice**:

1. While it is rarely better to file separate vice joint when married, it is still a good idea to run the numbers both ways to make sure you get the best results. Unmarried couples living together with their kids should run all the scenarios within the bounds of the law (who claims the kid, who gets Head of Household) to get the best results possible.

2. Do not miss out on Head of Household if you meet the rules (discussed earlier) since it has serious advantages. Parents can sometimes qualify you for it, even if they do not live with you. If you have a child that lives with you more than half of the year, but your custody agreement says the non-custodial parent gets to claim them, you still get Head of Household! Properly grant the other parent the ability to claim the child using Form 8332 and make sure they know to tell their preparer or their software that the child does NOT live with them more than half the year.

3. Joint custody parents with multiple children can often manipulate living situations to allow BOTH parents to claim Head of Household but be careful with this and do not lie about it. There should be an underlying reason why the children do not have the same living arrangements as each other.

# Most People Got a Tax Break in the Trump Law

The law was almost universally positive for all but a very few taxpayers. This does not mean it was a good law (or a bad law) just that the vast majority of people paid less taxes under the new regime.

This did not mean refunds improved. The IRS adjusted withholding tables, which should have distributed these savings to you via your paycheck, with each check being slightly bigger. People tended to pay attention to their refund, but the effect of this bill was in the amount of taxes that the IRS kept before sending your refund, not the refund itself.

At the end of 2019, a new W-4 Form was unveiled that finally eliminated the use of exemptions to calculate taxes. This Form also seemed to be driving toward smaller refunds, but with a lower chance of a balance due. More on this form later, but the trend seems to be that the powers that be want people to have more money in their paychecks, and less on their refunds.

Based on very limited and anecdotal information, I can confirm that most of my client's refunds were slightly lower on their 2018 and 2019 tax returns, even though most people's overall taxes went down. This was easy to see for clients with no major life changes and no adjustments made by the taxpayer to their withholding.

**My Advice**: Always focus on the bottom-line amount of taxes that the IRS kept and your "effective" tax rate. The effective tax rate is your total taxes divided by your income subject to tax (total income before any deductions used to determine your AGI). This is a FAR better comparison than your refund or balance due. That said, obsessing about taxes is not the best use of your time, beyond ensuring you get all your deductions and credits.

# Standard Deduction, Itemizing and Exemptions

I covered a lot of this earlier, but I am leaving it here for a refresher since the next few chapters will depend heavily on understanding this.

Everyone can either take a "Standard" deduction, based on their filing status, or prove that they have more "Itemized" deductions than the standard one. Then they deduct the bigger number – either taking the Standard Deduction or Itemizing. There are some deductions that you get without itemizing, such as student loan interest, but we will talk about those later. In addition to the standard deduction, you used to get an "exemption" for everyone you claimed as a dependent. This was $4050 in 2017.

Once you took all your deductions, you had "taxable income" and you figured the "tax" on this amount, usually using the tax tables, and sometimes special rates such as for capital gains.

Then you got "credits". These credits directly reduce the tax amount. These are much better than deductions or exemptions. Most credits cannot get your tax amount below zero, but some, "refundable" credits can actually reduce your tax below zero and get you back more money than you paid in!

For certain dependents, essentially children under the age of 17, you get a Child Tax Credit ($1000 before the new bill). Before the new law passed, all of it could be refundable for most people.

The next few chapters will go over the changes to the Standard Deduction, Exemptions, Child Tax Credit and Itemized Deductions.

# The New Standard Deductions

**UPDATE for 2020 ONLY**: As part of the CARES Act in response to the Coronavirus, non-itemizers (people who take the standard deduction as discussed below) can deduct up to $300 on top of their standard deduction for cash contributions to qualified charities. Qualified charities were not redefined, nor were requirements for documentation. Simply put, if you donate cash, check, online payment, credit card etc. to a charity that would normally qualify for a deduction if you itemized, you can deduct up to $300 in addition to your standard deduction without having to itemize deductions. This does not apply to contributions of "stuff" such as to Goodwill. Make sure to save proof of payment AND if the individual donation was more than $250, you need a written acknowledgment from the charity. This requirement is easily avoided by making two separate, smaller donations on different days. In that case proof can be as simple as a cancelled check, bank statement or credit card receipt or bill.

**January 2021 UPDATE**: The above deduction now applies to 2021 as well, and the limit went up to $600 for 2021. There is also a new penalty of 20% of the tax savings for 2020 and 50% for 2021 if you lie about donating to get this deduction.

The changes to the Standard Deduction will affect everyone and are one of the most dramatic changes the Trump Tax Bill made to tax rules. The changes seem pretty amazing, but they are not all that they appear to be:

The numbers in the next couple of paragraphs are all from 2018 and have changed since then. I am using them to illustrate the direct effect of the law. You will know when I have moved onto current numbers – because I will announce it clearly by stating "2020 Standard Deductions."

The Standard Deduction is based on filing status, which we have already covered. The Single (S) and Married Filing Separately (MFS) Standard Deduction went from $6,350 to $12,000 (but remember – MFS Standard Deduction starts at zero if the other spouse itemizes). Head of Household (HH) went from $9,350 to $18,000. Married Filing Jointly (MFJ) and Qualifying Widower (QW) went from $12,700 to $24,000. This means a lot of people who used to itemize will be taking the standard deduction. This is one of the big reasons that this bill is spoken of as "simplifying" the tax code. The additions for being over 65 and blind were left unchanged.

Here is the catch…as we will see in the next section, they eliminated the $4050 exemption for EVERYONE. Since everyone filing a tax return got an exemption (except people being claimed as dependents) this means S, QW, MFS and HH filers lost $4050 in exemptions, and MFJ lost $8100 in exemptions (one for the taxpayer and one for the spouse).

So, the actual effective change was:

Single went from $10,400 to $12,000
HH from $13,400 to $18,000
MFJ from $20,800 to $24,000.

HH looks pretty good, unless their dependent is 17 or over. In that case the loss of the Child Tax Credit effectively eliminates most of the benefit from the increase in Standard Deduction.

People with a LOT of itemized deductions are one of the categories of people who might do worse under the new plan – and this section gives you an idea why.

As I mentioned, the new standard deductions listed are for 2018. They will be adjusted for inflation going forward, so they will go up slightly every year. If you are close to the standard deduction, but still below it, grouping deductions you can manipulate (such as charity) into a single year, while taking the standard deduction in other years, is a way to maximize the effect of those deductions. I personally try to itemize every 3 years.

One of the major effects of these tax law changes that has come to light is the fact that claiming someone who is 17 or older is very often a matter of EXACTLY a $500 change in refund, since there is no exemption. Obviously, if there are education credits, Head of Household issues or Earned Income Credit, they can make a big difference, but in a ton of cases, it is $500. This really helps to put iffy situations into perspective. Claiming your adult brother, your girlfriend, your cousin etc., is usually a matter of $500. Now $500 bucks is 500 bucks, but is it really worth the potential hassle for just $500? Only you can answer that, and I am not trying to imply that it's not worth it. I'm just making the point that in a lot of situations, we can now put a very specific number on the value of a random, non-disabled, adult dependent.

Another unique fact about the elimination of the exemption is that someone claiming you generally does not affect your taxes, whereas before, only one person got your exemption (the $4050 deduction). This meant if you were claimed, you had potentially $4050 more of income to pay taxes on. Under the new law, unless you have education credits, your own children or something else weird, being claimed is no big deal. As a tax professional, I really love this change, because adults and their children have wildly differing ideas on who "supports" who, despite the tax laws being pretty clear on the matter. I have already seen a helpful de-escalation of conflicts between semi-adult children and their parents. Hopefully, me pointing this out will help you navigate the claiming of adult children in your life.

The above paragraph is complicated by the Coronavirus stimulus payments. A child 17 or older gets their parents no extra stimulus if they are claimed and they get nothing either. If they file independent, claiming themselves, they get $1200, and the parents generally only lose $500, with the exception of credits discussed before. Since most people already filed in either 2018 or 2019, there is not a lot of room for strategy here. If you have not filed, taking stimulus payment for your child into account (while still following the law) is important. We also think that children claimed in 2019 who are not in 2020 will get the $1200 on their 2020 return.

**2020 Standard Deductions**:

Single: $12,400
Head of Household: $18,650
Married Filing Jointly: $24,800
Married Filing Separately: $12,400 (or zero if spouse itemizes)
Qualifying Widower: $24,800

**My Advice**:

1. If you are close to the standard deduction every year, but not quite over it, consider grouping deductions that you control into a single year, and then taking the standard deduction every other year. Property taxes, medical bills and charity are the obvious ones here, especially Goodwill type charity. I describe the optimal strategy as one where you take the standard deduction every year, accumulating stuff until you are one bad weekend away from an episode of Hoarders, and then giving away everything you own to a Goodwill type charity all in one year where you also bundle up the tax payments you control. Matching this year to a high tax year, such as a year in which you sold appreciated stock, rental property or got a bonus will also make this strategy more powerful.

2. If claiming a dependent over 17 that does not make the difference between Head of Household and Single is shaky…let it go. Unless there are education credits or Earned Income Credit on the line, it is $500.

3. If you have not filed a 2018 or 2019 tax return, make sure you take stimulus payments into account when deciding who claims or does not claim someone. A professional's help will be key in this. We are going to talk about stimulus payments a lot in some later chapters, so if you don't feel like you have the data needed to make a decision…it is coming.

4. For 2020, save documentation of any cash-type donations to charity as discussed above to make sure you get your $300 deduction.

# Exemptions Are Eliminated and the New W-4

As was hinted at last chapter, the $4050 exemption for dependents and taxpayers is GONE. For the filers (taxpayer and spouse) it was made up for in the standard deduction increase. For children, it was made up for in the Child Tax Credit increase (next chapter). For other dependents and children 17 and over, it is only partially made up for.

The only real thing to discuss here is that the entire W-4 process that everyone is used to was based on exemptions (sort of). If you did not already know, the W-4 Form is how you tell your employer how much to withhold from your paycheck for taxes. You remember: Single and Zero, Married and 3, Married but Withhold at Higher Single Rate. All of that is gone. And good riddance! The old form was a sexist piece of crap that assumed the man made all the money and the woman stayed home and made babies. Any situation other than that and the form was completely useless. The new form is useful for a ton more situations, though not all. The good news is that the IRS created a Tax Withholding Estimator to complement the W-4, and it looks like it will work very well – if you use it right.

The new W-4 has 4 steps. The first step you identify your Filing Status: Married Joint, Married Separate or Single, and Head of Household. Step 2 has a bunch of stuff to read, but only one box to check – and it is a savior for many married couples. If you are married, and both of you work, check Box C in step 2. Unless your incomes are widely disparate, that box will fix everything for a two income household. Now comes the most important part of all: STOP. Do not fill out any more of the W-4 unless you are filling it out for the HIGHEST income source in the household. All kids, all credits, all extra income gets put on JUST ONE W-4 for the household. For the highest income W-4, Step 3 is for kids and other credits. Step 4 is where you identify any untaxed sources of money and/or ask for additional withholding to get a bigger refund or account for other issues.

Along with the new W-4 is the Tax Withholding Estimator. This allows you to use your paystubs for all the incomes in the household and input your tax situation in order to see how you look for tax results. I recommend using it in September or October to see where you are. Since it uses actual taxes already withheld, it gets more accurate later in the year, but you don't want to wait until there's not enough time to fix things. The plan is for it to also print out W-4's for all your jobs based on your desired refund amount, but that feature seemed to come and go early in 2020. Hopefully, it will be up and working for most of 2020.

One of the biggest downsides of the new W-4 is the inability to use the exemption number to make a small tweak. That said, the withholding calculator will be much more effective at fixing withholding, though it will usually do so by adding a fixed dollar deduction rather than an adjustment that changes with income. This means that as income increases, constant adjustment might be required. Using Step 4 additional income to artificially "boost" your income further into the higher brackets might be more sustainable. Strategies will develop better as the form gets more use.

Below is a link to the instruction page for the IRS withholding calculator. It includes instructions for how to get the most accurate results from using it. I am a BIG fan of utilizing the calculator!

https://www.irs.gov/individuals/tax-withholding-estimator

Below are links to the 2020 W-4 form, as well as the Frequently Asked Questions page for the new form at the Internal Revenue Service:

W-4:
https://www.irs.gov/pub/irs-pdf/fw4.pdf

FAQ's:
https://www.irs.gov/newsroom/faqs-on-the-2020-form-w-4

**My Advice:**

1. If you are a standard, married, two income family, each of you provide a new W-4 to your employer (or update online if your pay

system allows this). Check the Married Filing Joint box, and check Step 2 Box C. The higher income earner should account for children in Step 3.

2. If your income situation is unusual, and you are not happy with your current refund/balance due situation, working with a tax expert may be the best way to get the right W-4 input for your situation. The form has income tables and other tools that can be used, but they can be complicated to use. The tried and true method of tweak and see what happens is another technique you could use. This method calls for making a change to your W-4, seeing what happens to your paycheck, and then extrapolating the increase or decrease for a whole year, and then adjusting based on that. I am not a fan of that, since it doesn't automatically adjust for changes in income.

3. My best advice on the W-4 is what most people are going to hate. Establish a good baseline W-4 for all incomes based on the instructions and advice. Then get used to using the Tax Withholding Estimator accurately and use it regularly to check and tweak your W-4. It is relatively quick to use once you get used to it, and a 10-minute check every other month or so can work wonders. This is especially nice if you have the online ability to adjust your W-4, rather than having to hand the form into payroll or HR, who might get miffed at constant changes. I wouldn't worry about that too much since as you get things dialed in, you will eventually be able to just check it once or twice a year, without needing to make adjustments.

# New Credits for Kids and Dependents

I want to include lots of details in this chapter, so I am going to lay out the rules as they exist at this time, and add how they used to be as notes, asides or parentheticals.

Up until the year your child turns 17, you get a $2,000 credit off of your taxes called the Child Tax Credit (CTC). (The credit was $1000 before Trump Tax.) This credit cannot reduce your taxes below zero, but once you hit zero, another credit immediately appears. This additional credit has a confusing name that makes no real sense—the name is a carryover from when the credit was different (it is called the Additional Child Tax Credit). Anyway, I prefer to treat it as an extension of the CTC. Basically, you can get $2,000 for every child you have under 17 with no limit on the number of children (there is an income limit, discussed later). You calculate your taxes, and then reduce them by all your credits, in a certain order (most are taken before the CTC, leaving a lot of it behind to potentially reduce your taxes below zero). You take whatever was not needed to get you to zero, and do a calculation based on your income to figure out how much you get back from the government even when you are already at zero taxes owed! Here is the fine print:

1. The credit phases out by $50 for every $1,000 your AGI exceeds $400,000 if MFJ, $200,000 for other filing statuses. Before Trump Tax the MFJ limit was $110,000 and the other filing statuses had similarly lower limits. This was one of the best changes in the new law, allowing a lot more people to take advantage of the credit.
2. Don't look for a loophole around age 17, there isn't one. This is one of the few times when there is no exception to the age rules. You get 16 years of Child Tax Credit per child, no more.
3. The child must live with you for at least 6 months and a day (they can be away at school, on vacation and other temporary absences and still count as living with you, they basically just can't be living with someone else).
4. You must claim the child as a dependent.
5. The credit can exceed your total taxes if your earned income (generally wages or business profit) exceeds $2,500. After reducing your taxes to zero, you take your earned income minus $2,500,

multiply it by 0.15, and take the smaller of that number, and the amount of credit that was left after you reduced your taxes to zero. There is a maximum of $1,400 per child that can be refundable.
6. Starting in 2016, refunds with refundable Child Tax Credit can take until after 2/27/18 to arrive.

Dependents who do not qualify for the $2000 credit now get a $500 credit. Remember that credits come directly off taxes, not income. The $500 credit is non-refundable so it cannot reduce taxes below zero. Prior to Trump Tax there was no credit for dependents who did not qualify for the $1000 Child Tax Credit, you just got the exemption deduction for them – which the law eliminated.

The rules for who qualifies as a dependent have not changed substantially.

Because of the elimination of exemptions just discussed, these improvements are not as awesome as they look. For children under 17, you essentially break even if you are in the 25% tax bracket (ignoring tax rate and bracket changes), do better in the 15% or below, and worse in the higher brackets. For other dependents, only those in the 10% or below brackets will see an improvement, all others will lose some money. Again, this is just taking the exemption and dependent credits into account in determining "break-even". Other aspects of the tax law change should help most people.

The child you claim MUST have a valid Social Security Number to get the refundable portion of the Child Tax Credit. This must be obtained by the due date of the return, including extensions, so if you are having difficulty getting a SSN for a new child (usually due to it being born overseas) make sure to file for an extension of time to file.

**My Advice:**

1. Do not claim kids you do not fully qualify to claim. Just don't do it.

2. Do not let people claim your children if they are not entitled to do so. It is not okay, and, as I see all the time, they will continue to do it even after you tell them to stop.

3. Pay attention to your children's ages and be prepared for the tax hit when they hit age 17: $1500 less in Child Tax Credit.

# Mortgage Interest Deduction Changes

This is an Itemized Deduction.

There were minor tweaks to the ability to deduct interest paid on a home loan. First, the good news: This only applies to mortgages acquired in 2018 or later. If you are already deducting mortgage interest, you can continue to deduct it as before.

For new mortgages, they lowered how big a mortgage you can deduct interest on. Previously, you could deduct mortgage interest on the first $1,000,000 of mortgage. They lowered this to $750,000. This seems like a big deal, but the MOST you can lose is a deduction on $250,000 of mortgage. If your mortgage is over $750,000 you basically ratio the mortgage interest based on the amount owed. It is way more complicated than that, but you honestly don't lose a ton compared to the previous rules.

To be clear, the deduction doesn't disappear if you finance a $751,000 home, you just have to do some math (using a tax form) to deduct the interest on only the first $750,000 of money financed. It is also not "per home". It is a TOTAL of $750,000.

Obviously as home prices and interest rates rise, the math gets worse on the "lost" $250,000.

They also eliminated the ability to deduct home equity debt taken out after purchase, so you can't buy a car with home equity and deduct the interest. This was a terrible idea anyway, so I'm glad they got rid of it. You can still deduct home equity debt if it is used to buy, build or improve a personal residence.

**Mortgage Insurance Premium:** I am adding this here since it kinda fits into the whole mortgage interest deduction discussion and that is the part of the tax return where it goes. This zombie deduction goes away and comes back all the time. They just cannot seem to kill it. The tax law changes included in the late 2019 budget bills reinstated the Mortgage Insurance Premium (MIP) deduction for both 2019 AND 2018. Then the COVID bills extended it through

2021. This allows you to deduct mortgage insurance payments you made during the year. You can also deduct upfront mortgage insurance included as part of your initial mortgage (though refinancing payments have to be spread over 7 years). This includes FHA and VA funding fees that you pay for those types of mortgages. These SHOULD be included on the 1098 form you receive from your mortgage company or mortgage servicer, but if you know you pay insurance, you should check to be sure. If it is not on the 1098, you can include it as long as you can get the exact amount and prove it (contact your mortgage company to get the exact amount). You can find the VA and FHA funding fees on your Master Settlement Statement from closing. The deduction starts phasing out over $100,000 of income for Married Filing Joint taxpayers.

## My Advice:

1. You need to track who owns or services your loans during the year and ensure you get a 1098 from every one of them, or that the 1098 from the final company includes everything (rare). You should have a good idea, if not an exact amount, of how much interest you paid during the year so you can reconcile this. Mortgages get sold all the time, especially new ones. Companies also change who services their mortgages, so even when it isn't sold you can run into trouble. A few years ago, USAA changed servicers, so their members needed two 1098s. Most people did not realize this. Luckily, for my clients, I could see their amounts from the prior year were way higher, so I could pull the string and figure out what happened.
2. Do not miss that the mortgage insurance premium deduction was retroactive to 2018. Make sure to check your tax return for 2018, especially if you bought a new home in 2018. Your 1098 form for 2018 probably did not have the amount of mortgage insurance on it, so you are going to have to chase this down with your mortgage company. If you deducted it in 2017, and are deducting it in 2019, you almost certainly would have been able to deduct it in 2018. Do not miss out just because finding the information is hard.
3. Completely unrelated to tax law changes, but, if you are a veteran with a disability rating, you should not be paying the VA funding fee on a VA mortgage. Make sure your closing attorney, mortgage company and/or real estate agent know this. If you do pay the

funding fee mistakenly, or you get a retroactive rating to back before the mortgage date, contact the mortgage company (not the VA) to get the money back or applied to your principal.

4. And a brand-new wrinkle to the above about VA mortgages and disability that came up TWICE this year with my clients. I had never considered it before, but it probably happens a lot. If you get out of the military, either by retirement or finishing service (or being kicked out if you retain your benefits) do NOT buy a home while on terminal leave. Your disability rating will be backdated to the day you ACTUALLY were separated, not the day you started terminal leave. One client this year paid a $10,000 VA Funding Fee that would have been refunded if he had bought the house 20 days later. Obviously if you are absolutely certain you will not be putting a disability claim in, you can ignore this advice.

# State and Local Income Taxes

This is an Itemized Deduction.

They did not change what kind of state and local taxes you can deduct. Essentially, you can still deduct state and local property taxes and income taxes (or sales tax instead). They did, however, limit the amount you can deduct as an itemized deduction to a total of $10,000 ($5,000 if Married Filing Separately). This does not apply to businesses or rental property claimed on Schedules C and E, or other business returns, just itemized deductions. This will hurt in states with high income or property taxes. This will also affect more people over time, since it is not inflation adjusted.

One very useful strategy to look at is checking the amount you pay in both state income taxes AND sales tax. If both result in going over $10,000, you are better off taking sales tax, since you have to add back as income a state tax refund if you deducted income taxes (this will almost certainly not be true since they will have to come up with a way to ensure you don't pay taxes on something you didn't deduct, but using sales tax skips this issue completely). You can either save every receipt and add up your sales tax amount or use a convenient table the IRS provides that uses state, income and family size to provide you a number that you are allowed to use.

The IRS has been very effective in closing loopholes that many states have been creating to try and get around these limits. They, and Congress, have also implemented some things to undo the damage some people have had done to them by trying to use some of these loopholes, now closed (like making charitable deductions to your government vice taxes). See a tax expert if you are considering, or have used, some of these loopholes.

This does NOT impact deducting of taxes for business and rental property. It ONLY affects Itemized Deductions.

**My Advice:** You can safely manipulate when you pay car taxes if the end of the year falls within the billed date and due date of the taxes. Real Estate taxes are a little more shaky, but I still believe that if you get billed in November or December and it is not due until January, that you can safely "double up" on these taxes in an itemizing year by paying one early and one just on time. You would do this in conjunction with moving Medical and Charitable deductions into a single year when you "go for it" on itemizing because you normally fall below the standard deduction.

# Let's Talk About Disasters and COVID-19! (formerly Casualty and Thefts)

This is an Itemized Deduction (though now a ton of extra stuff is included here).

This post is not comprehensive or in full detail. I have tried to include and explain to the maximum extent necessary for the average taxpayer. If this post leads you to think you can use the benefits, you should talk to a tax pro or research the actual law. For the love of all that is holy, do NOT rely on your software to get this right. I use some of the best tax software in the world for my clients and I will be watching it like a hawk to make sure it gets this right (it is not – but I have been making it work by manipulating my form entries such that the software spits out an accurate tax return that accounts for all these provisions.) I have not included provisions that only apply to good sized businesses or employers.

I have used Big Letters to identify when I am switching between Tax Changes, since this chapter has a lot of them. Some of these provisions rightly belong as a part of other chapters, and I included relevant information in them, but the bulk of everything included in the various bills is written about here as well. If I don't move on to a new Capital Letter, you are still reading things that apply to the specific law or set of disasters.

## A. Trump Tax:

The Trump Tax Law Change to this was short and sweet, but it was a big deal. After that, Congress kept tweaking the rules for specific disasters or timeframes. I am going to cover each of them separately, even though a lot of it is going to be repetitive.

The basic rule established by the Trump Tax Law that applies to all disasters that do not have specific rules applied to them is this: Casualty losses are now only deductible if the loss was attributable to a disaster declared by the President.

The only real advice related to this is to make sure you have home/car/renter's insurance that is solid and up to date. Which you already should have.

The below is NOT an itemized deduction:

For disasters that occurred in 2016 ONLY: If you suffered unreimbursed losses that are attributable to one of the disasters that occurred in 2016, you can deduct these losses from your tax return as long as the loss exceeded $500. You don't need to itemize to do this (it can come on top of the standard deduction). The normal limitations for casualty loss deductions do not apply.

## B. The Sneaky Tax Change included in the Budget Bills in December of 2019:

Congress has played around with these provisions A LOT. In December 2019, mixed in with the budget bill were the below described provisions. Read carefully, they apply in very specific periods, but a LOT of people will qualify for some of them. This is not a comprehensive list of changes, but is trimmed down to those provisions most likely to apply to normal people:

To determine if your disaster qualifies, you go to the FEMA website:

https://www.fema.gov/disasters

Search for "Major Disaster Declaration" under Declaration Type and narrow it with your state.

I included the SC Dorian page here for illustration...

https://www.fema.gov/disaster/4464#

...so you can see the map. If you are in the orange area, most of the rules apply to you. A few more esoteric rules require you to be in a red area (not applicable to Dorian in SC). The disaster declaration must have been made between Jan 1st, 2018 and Feb 18th, 2020 and the disaster must have started before December 20th, 2019. These dates are on the FEMA pages.

Once you know the disaster applies to you, you can see what tax benefits you have. There are retirement account benefits, deductions, Child Tax Credit (EITC and ACTC) benefits, filing deadline extensions and charitable deduction provisions. The charity provisions apply to everyone who donates to the disasters, not just those affected by them.

**Retirement Provisions**: These generally require you to have suffered an economic loss as a result of the disaster, though it does not seem that the limits are tied to the amount of loss. Simply put, you would need losses that were not reimbursed by insurance - but check with your tax dude to confirm you qualify before futzing with your retirement accounts. I am going to use 401k here, but I mean all the 403b, Thrift Savings Plan, 457 etc. deferred compensation type plans.

1. You can avoid the 10% penalty on an early 401k or IRA withdrawal. The max is $100,000 per disaster. The withdrawal must be made after the disaster began and 60 days after 12/27/2020. You still have to pay taxes on the withdrawal but...

2. You can spread the taxes over three years starting with the year you took it out. Or...

3. You can put the money back within 3 years of the distribution date and owe no taxes.

4. If you took advantage of the normal $10,000 first time home buyer exclusion but the disaster prevents you from buying or building the home, you can put the money back tax and penalty free. The withdrawal must have been made within 180 days before the disaster and 30 days after it ended. The money must be put back before June 17th, 2020.

5. The 401k loan allowed amount was doubled to $100,000. Payments due between the start of the disaster and 180 days after may be delayed until June 17th, 2020.

**Disaster Loss Deduction**: The rules for a disaster loss deduction are modified to eliminate the 10% floor and to allow the deduction to be taken even if you do not itemize. Basically, you take your losses, subtract any insurance reimbursement, subtract $500 (the new floor) and that is the amount deducted. If you itemize, just include it as an itemized deduction. If you do not, add it to your standard deduction. Make sure your software or tax pro handles this right.

Very rough, even number example: Say your standard deduction is $12,000 and your house has $10,000 in damage done. Insurance reimburses $5000. So, your deduction is $10,000 minus $5000, minus $500 which equals $4,500. If you take the standard deduction, it would now be $16,500. If you had $15,000 in itemized deductions, the disaster loss would now make them $19,500.

**Earned Income Credit and Additional Child Tax Credit**: Here's where things get really weird. If your principal abode was in the disaster area, or you were displaced due to the disaster (these are weird so ask a pro if your home wasn't in the zone) and your earned income went DOWN, you can use the prior year's earned income in these calculations if it works out better. You basically have to run the numbers both ways to see which way is best. You can do this for any year that falls within the disaster dates. You have to use the prior year's income for BOTH credits or neither.

For Married Filing Jointly, only one spouse needs to be affected, but you have to use BOTH spouses' income from the prior year for the calculation.

I cannot see anything requiring the disaster to be the CAUSE of the reduced income.

For 2020 tax returns, ANYONE can use 2019 income to calculate ALL of Earned Income Tax Credit, Child Tax credit and Additional Child Tax Credit. You have to apply 2019 income to all of these or none of them. You can't pick and choose. Make sure your software or preparer has 2019 numbers to check this.

**Filing Deadline Extension**: You get a 60-day extension of any filing deadline that falls between the start and end of the disaster. The 60 days starts after the disaster is over. It applies to IRA contribution deadlines as well. It only applies to disasters occurring AFTER December 20th, 2019.

**Charitable Contributions**: These changes were superceded by Coronavirus tax bills.,

## C. Coronavirus Tax Provisions:

This section includes most of the tax law changes and other Treasury department action up through December of 2020. Since COVID has dominated tax law changes lately, some of the tax provisions from the very latest relief bill (the one with $600 stimulus checks) are covered elsewhere either in addition, or instead of this chapter.

**Retirement Provisions:** You do not have to take your 2020 Required Minimum Distribution from your Retirement Account. This applies to people over the age of 70 and a half who have to take annual withdrawals from their tax advantaged accounts and pay taxes on them. This is an under-reported and under-appreciated big deal. I highly recommend taking advantage of this if you do not need the money from your account. Pulling money out during a dramatic stock market downturn is painful. People who inherited IRA money who are pulling it out as required over 5 years can extend this period by one additional year.

If you suffered economic impact from the Coronavirus, specifically, you or a family member you care for contracted the disease, or you lost your job or lost business or were laid off, or lost business income due to the virus, or your child's daycare closing caused you financial hardship, you can withdraw up to $100,000 from your retirement accounts without penalty and with the ability to pay the taxes due over three years, or put the money back and pay no taxes. The connection and calculations between the economic impact and the withdrawal amounts are not clearly defined. The period to make withdrawals was extended into late February 2021.

Retirement plan loan limits were increased from $50,000 to $100,000 and you do not have to start paying it back for a year. This applies to loans taken between March 27th and September 23rd of 2020.

There are also changes to loan requirements and costs associated with making a hardship withdrawal. I DO NOT recommend doing this unless ABSOLUTELY necessary and only withdraw the minimum amount possible to keep your family alive. In fact, there are so many programs available to defer rent, mortgages and student loan payments that this should not be necessary.

**Time Extensions and Suspension of Enforcement**: You do not have to pay your balance due for 2019 until 7/15/2020. Most states are following suit. You also do not have to make your first or second Estimated Tax Payment for 2020 until 7/15/2020. If you scheduled a direct debit before then, you may cancel the payment by calling the IRS. Here is what they say about it: "Call IRS e-file Payment Services 24/7 at 1-888-353-4537 to inquire about or cancel your payment, but please wait 7 to 10 days after your return was accepted before calling. Cancellation requests must be received no later than 11:59 p.m. ET two business days prior to the scheduled payment date." The above extension now applies to nearly all categories of tax returns.

The IRS has suspended pulling back taxes, delinquent student loans and other debts from tax refunds and stimulus payments. Delinquent Child Support withdrawals are still happening on a state by state basis.

**Charitable Giving**: For 2020 only, you can deduct $300 of cash, check or equivalent donations to normally qualified charities even if you do not itemize. You can deduct up to your entire AGI in charitable donations via itemizing, as opposed to the normal limit. Documentation requirements remain the same: donations under $250 require some record of your paying it, such as a cancelled check or credit card statement while $250 or above requires written acknowledgement from the charity. The $250 limit applies to INDIVIDUAL donations, not the total amount donated for the year.

The above was modified with the latest relief bill to allow a similar deduction of up to $600 in 2021. It also clarified that a penalty of 20% of tax benefit applies if you lie about donating in 2020. The penalty is 50% for 2021.

**Health Savings Accounts and Flexible Spending Accounts**: HSA, FSA and MSA funds may now be used for over-the-counter medications. They may also be used for menstrual care products. This change is permanent. Employers may extend leftover money in FSA accounts through 2021 rather than the money being surrendered. Childcare money can be used for children up to age 13 in 2021 ONLY vice the usual age of 12.

**Student Loans**: There are a number of student loan deferment programs implemented that are beyond the scope of taxes, but one is tax related. That one allows an employer to pay up to $5,250 of your student loans between March 27th and the end of 2025 without it being taxable income to you. You cannot deduct the interest paid by your employer.

**Business Rule Changes**: I am going to cover Sick and Family Leave credits that apply to businesses and self-employed individuals in the next chapter, but, these aside, most of these go beyond the scope of this book, applying mainly to employers or not being tax related. A non-exhaustive list includes the ability of self-employed people to collect unemployment for business income reduction, the ability to postpone paying payroll taxes, a dollar-for-dollar credit against payroll taxes for paying employees on sick leave, the ability to carry back 2018 to 2020 net operating losses, increased business interest deduction allowed, accelerating credits for prior year AMT, and numerous credits for retaining employees or paying for sick leave. There was also a permanent correction to allow immediate expensing of improvement property by making it a 15-year depreciable item.

**Self-Employment Tax**: Self employed taxpayers can defer 6.2% (half of the Social Security portion of Self Employment Tax). They don't have to pay it while filing their 2020 tax return and can account for it when calculating Estimated Tax Payments. If you underpaid your estimated payments, this MIGHT help you avoid some penalties. You have to repay half of the deferred amount by 12/31/2021 and the other half by 12/31/2022.

**Payroll Tax Holiday**: Trump authorized the delay in payment of Social Security taxes through the end of 2020. The deferred payments will be recouped through the end of 2021. I don't think many employers took advantage of this, except the military and Federal employees. If you had these taxes deferred make sure that you are prepared for your employer to start taking extra amounts out in January 2021. Your employer should be providing detailed information on how this will work. If you changed employers, you are responsible for repaying these taxes.

**Things I do not know jack about**: There is greatly expanded ability to get unemployment benefits if you have reduced income vice full job loss, and for self-employed people. There are amazing small business loan opportunities, some of which do not require paying back (go to sba.gov). There are programs that limit the ability to evict people based on non-payment of rent, guaranteed deferment of mortgage payments for government backed loans, and deferment of student loan payments.

**IRS Operations**: At the time of publishing the original version of this book in March of 2020, the IRS had suspended a significant amount of operations. They were not manning phone lines, many fax lines were turned off and they were not processing ANY paper tax returns, including amendments. Almost all local service centers were closed. Even the Taxpayer Advocate Service was operating on a very limited basis. They had just started resuming limited operations to try to clear the backlog, but, if you are struggling getting a return processed by the IRS, it is likely to be a long time before it is handled. Getting assistance with anything that cannot be handled using an automated phone line or online tool was simply impossible.

As of December 2020, most operations were still operating in a limited fashion, though much better than early in the Pandemic.

**A bunch of links on my blog**: There are a bunch of useful resources out there. I linked to a bunch of them on this post (there's some politics and news in there as well:

https://supertaxgenius.blogspot.com/2020/04/the-big-coronavirus-link-post.html

**My Advice**:

1. Do not use the exemptions as an excuse to liquidate your retirement account. It is still the best place for your money. If you need to make a withdrawal to SURVIVE, make it the smallest possible amount to keep the lights on, rent paid and food on the table. If you take the money out and do not put it back in the timeframe specified, the only exemption is on the 10% penalty. You still pay taxes on the whole amount. Keep in mind that plans tend to grossly under withhold on these types of withdrawals, so talk to your tax guy or gal before making the withdrawal so they can give you a good number to withhold.
2. Likewise, the expanded list of Health Savings Account qualified purchases should not motivate you to use your HSA more. Use your HSA only for truly unaffordable health costs, and let that sucker grow into your retirement.
3. Check irs.gov and my blog at least weekly for updates to the above information, as well as details of any new rules or laws passed.
4. Keep proof of all cash type donations even if you do not normally itemize.
5. Document economic costs you suffer from COVID-19, even if you do not currently qualify for any relief. We do not know what benefits may come AND you might be forced to withdraw from your retirement for other reasons, and COVID-19 economic losses will provide access to a number of benefits.
6. Seek professional assistance from financial advisors and tax professionals if you think some of the more complex rules might apply to you BEFORE taking irrevocable actions.

7. Until the Coronavirus Pandemic has passed, try to do as much as possible regarding taxes electronically.

# If You Are Self Employed and Can't Work

**Read this chapter if you suffered ANY work or business interruption due to COVID to make certain if you are or are not entitled to some tax benefits.**

If you are unable to work or engage in your business as a result of quarantines, shutdowns, getting sick, school/daycare closings or various other reasons, you might be entitled to one or both of credits for sick leave or family leave. These credits are for employers to recoup payments they make to their employees who are unable to work for the above reasons. But, if you would have been entitled to these credits as an employee doing what you do, you qualify for them as the employer of yourself. In this case the government pays you for being unable to work for yourself.

Exactly how to define what makes the work you do qualifying as an employee is a bit nebulous, but it seems like a fairly liberal interpretation is appropriate, so I would go into conversations with you tax guy assuming you might qualify, and have the information required for them to calculate the credit rather than waiting to find out if you qualify. There were ways to get this money in advance, by reducing estimated payments, but it's pretty much too late for that to be effective, though you can reduce your Estimated Payment due on January 15th to account for the amount of credit you are entitled to. Either way, you claim the credit on your 2020 tax return and it reduces your balance due or increases your refund.

This sucker gets complicated, so I'm going to start with a link to the IRS FAQ on the subject:

https://www.irs.gov/newsroom/special-issues-for-employees#specific-provisions-related-self-employed-individuals

I'm going to try my best to simplify how these work, but you absolutely need professional help to get these right. After discussing the various credits, I'm going to list the information you want to have available for when you file taxes. That will replace the "My Advice" section that is usually at the end of every chapter.

## Qualified Sick Leave Wages Credit:

1. You get up to 10 days worth of this credit.
2. If YOU are unable to work or telework because the government shut you down, ordered a quarantine, a doctor quarantined you due to being exposed, you had symptoms and were waiting for a diagnosis, or you actually had the disease you are entitled to $511 per day or 100% of your average daily earnings, whichever is lower, for each day you could not work.
3. If you cannot work because you are caring for SOMEONE ELSE due to conditions similar to the above, or due to the closing of a school, daycare or other facility, or your daycare provider is unable to work, you are entitled to $200 per day or 67% of your average daily earnings, whichever is lower, for each day you could not work.
4. Average daily earnings are your net earnings from your business in either 2019 or 2020 (whichever is more) divided by 260. You get this number when you prepare your taxes as the bottom line on Schedule C.
5. If you received sick wages as an employee with a regular job, you have to reduce these credits by the amount of wages you were paid while not working (no double dipping).
6. This credit is not counted as income, even though it technically replaces income.
7. This applies to sick leave through 3/31/2021.

## Qualified Family Leave Wages Credit:

1. This is VERY similar to the situation described in 3 above, but basically takes over where the 10 days above end.
2. You get 50 days worth of this credit.
3. You get this credit for any day you would have been qualified for Family Leave wages due to COVID if you were an employee (basically the situation described in 3 above). You are entitled to $200 per day or 67% of your average daily earnings, whichever is lower, for each day you could not work.
4. Average daily earnings are your net earnings from your business in 2019 or 2020 (whichever is higher) divided by 260. You get this number when you prepare your taxes as the bottom line on Schedule C.

5. If you received family leave wages as an employee with a regular job, you have to reduce these credits by the amount of wages you were paid while not working (no double dipping).
6. This credit is not counted as income, even though it technically replaces income.
7. This applies to sick leave through 3/31/2021.

**Information you should provide to your tax dude:**

1. Proof, as best you can get, of the situations discussed above. This could be doctor's notes, notices from schools or daycare facilities, quarantine or shutdown notices, COVID test results, copies of government statements regarding allowed working conditions, or even newspaper articles reporting on work rules and quarantines.
2. The number of days you were unable to work due to YOU being affected by quarantines, shutdowns etc. as previously discussed.
3. The number of days you were unable to work due to caring for someone else as a result of quarantines, closures etc. as discussed previously.
4. The detailed reasons you were unable to work or make money for the days discussed above.

# Hopefully, You Already Have Your Stimulus Money…

**UPDATE November 2020**: At this point, if you don't have your original stimulus payment, there is very little you can do other than electronically file a 2020 tax return. Because another stimulus is possible, and will likely follow the same rules, I am leaving the rest of this chapter unchanged. My best advice is to file a 2020 tax return electronically, even if not required to do so. Use direct deposit if possible. Use the best address you can that will ensure you get mail sent by the IRS. Update this address using Form 8822 if you move. This will ensure you have the highest likelihood possible of getting any new stimulus checks should they decide to send more. There should be many easy ways to file a tax return cheap (or free) next year if you usually don't have to file.

**UPDATE January 2020**: A second set of stimulus checks at an amount of $600 was passed. The details specific to this stimulus were covered in the first chapter after the introduction. Most of the information here applies to these new checks, though getting them should be a lot simpler since they worked the kinks out the first time.

**Here is the original chapter:**

Hopefully, you already have your stimulus money…

If not, or you are curious how it worked, this is the chapter for you! The information here changes almost daily, so keep checking irs.gov for updates. It is highly likely some of this will be out of date within minutes of publishing the book. I will update on my blog as things change:

www.supertaxgenius.com

## How much am I getting and what do I need to do?

For most people, the answer is $1,200 per taxpayer and spouse (each) and $500 for each dependent under age 17 and you don't need to do anything. Specifically, if you filed a 2019 tax return, made less than $75,000 filing Single or Married Filing Separately, $112,500

Head of Household, $150,000 Married Filing Jointly, and had direct deposit to an account that is still active, you will be getting a deposit in short order and don't need to do anything. If the last tax return you filed was 2018, and the above limits were met, you also will get the payment and do not need to do anything. If that is not the case, keep reading for details.

## Who will not get a payment?

People 17 or older who are claimed as a dependent.
Single or Married Filing Separately taxpayers who made more than $99,000 and had no children under 17.
Head of Household taxpayers who made more than $136,500 and had no children under 17.
Married Filing Joint taxpayers who made over $198,000 and had no children under 17.

You also will not get a payment if you did not file a 2018 or 2019 tax return and you take none of the actions described later (and you get none of the income sources discussed later). You will get what you deserve on your 2020 tax return, but you have to file at least a 2018, 2019 or 2020 tax return (or use the non-filer portal described later) to get a payment.

If you do not meet the criteria of the previous two paragraphs, you can use this calculator from H&R Block to get a good estimate of what you should receive:

https://www.hrblock.com/coronavirus-tax-impact/calculator/

## Who needs to do something?

**People who did not provide direct deposit information on their latest tax return:** This includes people who owed, regardless of if they used direct debit. The IRS has provided a portal for updating direct deposit information to get your check faster, otherwise it can take up to TWENTY weeks to get your check. The IRS will prioritize lower incomes for check mailing. More details on the Get My Payment portal below.

**People who did not file a 2018 or 2019 tax return.** File a return as soon as possible to get your tax return unless you receive Social Security, SSI, Railroad Retirement or VA disability and have it direct deposited AND you have no dependents and your spouse also receives one of the above. If not, see the instructions below on Getting a Payment if you did not file.

**People who filed a 2018 tax return and made too much money to qualify, or who have kids born in 2019**: File a 2019 tax return to make sure you get the full amount of the check. If you file 2019 after they calculate and send a stimulus check based on 2018, I don't think you will get an updated stimulus based on 2019. I do know they will recalculate on 2020 and pay you extra if you qualify for more, but won't make you pay back if you qualify for less.

**People who have closed or changed the bank account to which their last tax return was directed**: Use the Get My Payment portal to update direct deposit information. For some people this might not work and if your direct deposit bounces, they will mail you a check.

**People without a bank account who have moved**: Update your address with the IRS using Form 8822 ASAP!

**What if you aren't required to file and don't receive Social Security or other income sources listed in the previous paragraph?** You might want to file a "simple" return which the IRS says to do using $1 of interest labelled as "Stimulus Payment" as if it was received on a 1099INT. I have instructions for this below. If you have a W-2 but did not file because it did not result in a decent refund, you can file a return ASAP to get your money. The IRS says to file a $1 return or use the non-filer app to get a stimulus faster if you are not qualified for a refund based on your W-2. Check what your refund will be and then decide which system to use.

**What to do if you owe for 2019 and have not filed:** File your tax return ASAP and then use the Get My Payment portal discussed below to provide direct deposit information to the IRS. This will ensure your stimulus payment is dropped to that account and will be available to cover your balance due (or to spend).

**What happens if I don't file a 2018 or 2019 tax return, or made too much money on the latest filed tax return to qualify?** The payment is truly based on your 2020 tax return, so if you qualify for a payment but didn't get it (or qualify for a larger one) it will be provided on your 2020 tax return.

**Is the payment taxable? Do I have to pay it back? What if I make more money in 2020 such that I should not have qualified?** The payment IS an advance on your 2020 tax return, but the amount is from a BRAND-NEW credit that increases your 2020 tax return. It is not taxable; it does not have to be paid back. If you qualify for a bigger payment on your 2020 tax return, you get the extra. If you deserve less, they let it go.

The IRS will send you a letter detailing the amount you should have received and if it was a mailed check or a direct deposit. It will say it is from Donald Trump in the White House, but it is from the IRS. I got mine exactly 2 weeks after I received my payment, which was deposited on April 15th.

**Scams**: No one is going to call or email you requesting you provide direct deposit information, personal information or have you pay money upfront to get the payment. The scams have already started.

**Getting the Status of your Payment and Updating Direct Deposit Information:**

https://www.irs.gov/coronavirus/get-my-payment

You use this app if you filed a 2018 or 2019 tax return but did not have a REFUND direct deposited into your account. If you OWED...this is the app for you.

You can also use the app to get a status of your payment, even if you expect it to be deposited normally.

To use the app, you click on the blue "Get My Payment" button. Enter the primary taxpayer's SSN, birthday (with slashes) and the address from the last tax return filed. Make sure the address matches the return exactly - specifically - make sure to abbreviate or not abbreviate Rd, Street, etc as it appears on the return. Also, if you have apartment, it should look like: 10 State St #7 vice using APT or other words.

This will give you the status of your payment and tell you if the IRS needs direct deposit information. If it says information is not available, this usually means they have not processed a return on which to base your stimulus or they haven't updated the system. Check once a day for updates. Anecdotally, it appears that some small number of people are taking a long time to get updated in the system. Also, people who paper filed the tax return required to get a stimulus payment after the Coronavirus hit might have to wait a lot longer, because the IRS is currently not processing paper filed returns.

To provide direct deposit information, you enter the Adjusted Gross Income from your 2019 return (or 2018 if 2019 not filed), indicate if it was a refund or balance due on that return, and provide the amount of the refund or balance due. You enter your routing and account number twice, and then the IRS confirms that your deposit information has been updated.

It appears that it takes 1 to 2 weeks after updating your information to get a direct deposit. Updates made by 4/22/2020 got deposits on or before 4/30/2020. Looks like this once a week pattern continued.

Keep in mind that any delays processing your return will have a corresponding delay in getting information to the "Get My Payment" app and getting your stimulus deposit.

### Getting a Payment When You Did Not File a 2018 or 2019 Tax Return:

The IRS is going to send stimulus checks based on a 2019 or 2018 tax return. You might need to file a tax return in 2019 to get your stimulus check. Here are a few scenarios where it might be required and all of these assume you don't already have a 2018 tax return that has proper information for your income and direct deposit information:

Instead of doing the $1 returns below, the IRS now has a free non-filer system available at the link below:

https://www.irs.gov/coronavirus/non-filers-enter-payment-info-here

1. You made too little income in 2019 to require a tax return and are not claimed as a dependent in 2019. In this case, prepare a tax return using your income documents and provide direct deposit information for the refund. If the return says it cannot be filed due to no income, enter $1 on a 1099INT form (bank interest) and put "Stimulus Payment" as the bank name.
2. You receive Social Security, VA disability, SSI or Railroad retirement, but your spouse does not receive any of those or you have dependents. In this case, file a tax return (jointly if married) claiming all dependents. Enter $1 on a 1099INT form (bank interest) and put "Stimulus Payment" as the bank name. Obviously provide direct deposit information for the zero-tax return. The deadline for doing this passed on 5/5/2020. If you did not update your information by this time, you will have to wait until you file your 2020 tax return to get the extra money.
3. You have no reportable income (or have reportable income but are below the filing threshold and not due a significant refund) and are not claimed as a dependent. File a tax return and enter $1 on a 1099INT form (bank interest) and put "Stimulus Payment" as the bank name. Obviously provide direct deposit information for the zero tax return.

You don't need to file a return to get your stimulus if you, and your spouse, if married, receive Social Security (or Railroad retirement) and have it direct deposited and have no dependents. No action is required on your part in this situation. This also applies if you receive SSI or VA disability.

Most of the scenarios above will qualify for free filing using online software and many professional tax preparation companies are offering some of these tax returns fee free. You should NOT file a state return unless there is sufficient refund to justify the fees (assuming you do not have a state filing requirement, which you shouldn't if you're in need of this post). A state tax return is NOT required to get the stimulus payment.

**My Advice:**

1. A child over 17 on your tax return gets you $500. Filing independently, they could get $1200. So, some strategy is involved. It appears that a child claimed in 2019 that is not claimed in 2020 who files a tax return will get $1200, even if their parents got $500 in 2019. I believe this means they should file in 2020 even if not required. That said, you cannot just "decide" that your child is independent. They have to provide more than half of their own support. This means that your child filing a tax return independently with $4000 in income when they still live with you is probably not an accurate return.
2. Filing separately if one person has a big income and the other doesn't could get you a stimulus check when otherwise not entitled due to income, but will probably mess up your tax return results worse than the stimulus improvement – but it is worth checking.
3. If your 2018 tax return met the above requirements and your 2019 does not, and you have not filed 2019 yet, you should wait to file until after you get your stimulus payment.
4. Check irs.gov and my blog at least weekly for updates to the above information, as well as details of any new rules or laws passed.
5. The Treasury Secretary says that if you receive a stimulus check for someone who has died that you should return it. A lot of people, myself included, think that contradicts the law. I would wait for further guidance from the IRS before sending a check back (not that there's a mechanism for that anyway) and if the check is approaching its expiration date, I would deposit it and leave it while waiting on further guidance.
6. File a 2020 tax return even if not required to do so. Have it direct deposited and use an address that is likely to remain good for a while. Print a copy of the tax return for use if you need to update information due to moving or closing bank accounts. Do this even if you already got a Stimulus check. This is really just a pure paranoia move to make absolutely certain that any new stimulus money makes it to you as quickly as possible.

7. If you made too much money in 2019 to get a stimulus payment, but have the ability to change that in 2020, you need to pay attention to things like stock sales and other unique sources of income. A tax pro can be a big help on this.

# Gambling Losses and Charity

These are Itemized Deductions.

The Trump Tax Law changes were minor in nature. You can deduct gambling losses up to the amount of your winnings. The law clarifies that expenses other than gambling losses associated with gambling are subject to the same limit.

The only charitable contribution changes most people will care about from the Trump Tax Law are:

An increase in the percentage of your income you can deduct as charity (believe it or not you could only deduct half of your income as a charitable contribution, no matter how much you gave – the rest gets carried over to the next year). The law raised this to 60%. Be aware that some types of contributions, such as stock that has increased in value, are subject to stricter limits.

You cannot deduct a contribution if you receive the right to buy sporting event tickets due to the donation.

## For 2020 and 2021 ONLY (COVID-19 provisions):

The 60% limit is suspended for cash contributions. You can now deduct up to 100% of your AGI. This does not apply to non-cash, Goodwill type donations. Cash means check, credit card, online etc. Documentation requirements and qualified organizations remain unchanged.

As a result of the Coronavirus, you can deduct $300 (2020) or $600 (2021) of cash, check or equivalent donations to normally qualified charities even if you do not itemize. You can deduct up to your entire AGI in charitable donations via itemizing, as opposed to the normal limit. Documentation requirements remain the same: donations under $250 require some record of your paying it, such as a cancelled check or credit card statement while $250 or above requires written acknowledgement from the charity. The $250 limit applies to INDIVIDUAL donations, not the total amount donated for the year.

A penalty of 20% of tax proceeds for 2020 and 50% for 2021 applies if you lie about donating to get this credit.

**My Advice**:

1. Keep proof of all cash type donations even if you do not normally itemize. I recommend doing this for later years as well, since I think this might become a permanent and/or zombie provision.
2. If you want to donate more than $250, just make a smaller donation on two separate days. This means you just need your own records as proof of the donations, and avoids the need to get a letter or other acknowledgement from the charitable organization.

# Medical Expense Limit Change

This is an Itemized Deduction.
This is the never to be fully implemented zombie provision and it has FINALLY DIED! The late December 2020 relief bill ended the 10% limit for good!

You can deduct medical expenses, but several years ago, there was a floor, equal to 7.5% of your Adjusted Gross Income, below which you could not deduct them. It made sense, in that you did not want to have to keep receipts for every little thing, so the limit ensured you only deducted medical expenses if they really impacted your finances. The Affordable Care Act was phasing in a change to that limit, making it 10% for everyone except people near 65 years and older.

For 2017 and 2018, the limit was dropped back to 7.5%. For 2019 and beyond, the 10% threshold applies...or does it?

NOPE – it is 7.5% for the foreseeable future.

I hope you didn't throw away all those medical receipts because they didn't hit the 10% threshold!

## My Advice:

1. Keep proof of all medical expenses even if you do not normally itemize or hit the 7.5% threshold. Don't add them up unless you are sure you will meet the requirements, but saving documentation is important not just because they keep changing the rules, but if you suffer an expensive medical condition late in the year, all those little receipts might become deductible.

# Miscellaneous Itemized Deductions

These are Itemized Deductions (in case the title didn't clue you in).

ALL the miscellaneous itemized deductions subject to the 2% floor have been repealed. These are, in rough descending order of significance and only including ones that aren't totally obscure:

Employee Business Expense (when you pay for things or drive for your job)
Depreciation of Computer Used to Invest
Fees to Collect Interest and Dividends
Hobby Expenses
Investment Fees and expenses
Loss on IRA's after all Funds are Distributed
Safe Deposit Box Fees
Service Charges on Dividend Reinvestment Plans
Tax Preparation Fees and Expenses
Union Dues*
Educator Expenses (except the $250 non-itemized deduction) *
Boomer Deduction*
Rural Mail Carriers Vehicle Expense*
Employee Travel Expense*
Work Clothes and Uniforms*
Work Related Education*
Repayments of Social Security Benefits
Research Expense of College Professor

*These are all Employee Business Expenses, but I thought I would state them separately for clarity. Some of these will be discussed in more detail later as they apply to specific situations.

People still struggle with the idea that you simply do NOT get ANY deductions as an employee unless they are specifically called out in another section. People who work from home, truck drivers and people who drove for work were devastated by these changes. Anecdotally, it appears that employers are not stepping up to fill in the gap this has been created, at least for current employees. If you are negotiating for a new job that involves significant personal expenses, make sure to take that into account during when discussing salary or reimbursement.

One way to ensure you don't bear employment expenses out of pocket is for your employer to reimburse them under an "accountable plan". This makes the payments tax-free to you, and deductible by your employer. An accountable plan simply means they pay you in advance or reimburse you for actual expenses, properly accounting for them within 60 days to ensure you receive reimbursement for things you paid for or pay back any excess advances. There is some slop to the 60 days, but your employer needs to figure out their plan's timeframes and make sure it complies with the rules. Most things require an exact dollar for dollar amount, but they can reimburse you a standard mileage rate or federally established daily meal rate.

It is important to understand that some of these deductions mirror deductible expenses of business owners as opposed to employees. They have only been eliminated for employees. If you own a business, most of these are still deductible on your business return. There is a lot more information on businesses available further into the book.

**A Coronavirus Comment**: This change has particular application during the COVID-19 Pandemic. Before this change, working from home could result in a number of deductions for home office, travel, supplies, ZOOM subscriptions and many other things. NONE of these are deductible for an employee, even if COVID has forced them to work from home. A self-employed person might be able to deduct all of these things, but the Trump Tax Law eliminated ALL employee business deductions.

**My Advice**:

1. Try to get your employer to establish an accountable plan as discussed above.
2. Spread the word that employee expenses are no longer deductible so people stop saving receipts and spending money on stuff just because they think they can deduct it.

3. If COVID forced you to work from home, try to get your employer to pay for as much as possible, but also recognize that, while expenses at home might have increased, commuting expenses and frustration likely decreased.

## Corporate Tax Rate

The Trump tax Law cut the tax rate for corporations 21 percent. This and the 20 percent business taxable income deduction discussed in the next chapter, were intended to make having a business in the United States more attractive.

They are also intended to make corporate and other business tax rates closer to each other.

That is about all I'm going to say on the subject, because I'm guessing corporations have experts they're using to do their taxes, as opposed to this book.

There are major changes to how foreign income is taxed that are designed to bring businesses and income back to the U.S. I am NOT going into those, so this chapter is pretty fricken' short.

# 20% Business Deduction

The next few paragraphs of this section will cover how the Trump Tax Law changes affected the vast majority of businesses. The rest is for people making a lot of money (relatively speaking). Income limitations are for 2020 unless otherwise noted.

This has been called the "pass-through" deduction, but that's not really accurate. It includes almost all business income, including sole-proprietorships, S corporations, limited liability companies and income from investments in publicly traded partnerships and real estate investment trusts. There is also a possibility that it applies to residential rental property, as discussed next

As far as rental property is concerned, it will be a "facts and circumstances" determination. If it is a business, based on "facts and circumstances" then it will be eligible for the deduction. Obviously, someone renting a former house out using a property manager probably will not qualify, but the more time spent on rentals, and the more businesslike it is run, the more likely it is to be eligible. Since most rentals start out at a loss, and these losses must be accounted for before eligible for the deduction, it seems most small landlords will find it more trouble than it's worth. That said, a decision needs to be made early The IRS has established "Safe Harbor" rules to allow you to use the deduction for rental properties without worrying about your circumstances being disputed. They require that you perform 250 hours per year on "rental services". This is pretty hard to meet for a single rental. Services include maintenance, cleaning, rent collection, paperwork, legal efforts, advertising, finding tenants and pretty much anything else involved in managing the property. Efforts to find new property, and related efforts such as gathering or arranging financing, do not count. You must maintain separate records for the rental, and they must be "contemporaneous" meaning you maintain them in real time, vice reconstructing at a later date. If the rental has been in existence for more than four years, you only have to meet the test in three of the prior five years including the year in question.

There are a lot of weird provisions that kick in above a certain income, but if your TAXABLE* income (income after virtually all deductions other than this one) is less than $163,300 ($326,600 Married Filing Jointly (MFJ)), then this pretty much applies to all business income and you get to deduct 20% of your net profit from each business directly off of your taxable income. This is designed to cause all businesses to pay about the same tax rate as corporations do with the new lower corporate rate.

Above those numbers, a lot of weirdness kicks in.

If your business is service oriented** and your taxable income is over $163,300 ($326,600 MFJ), then your deduction starts to phase out and will be completely gone at $213,300 ($426,600 MFJ).

If your taxable income is $163,300 ($326,600 MFJ) and you have a non-service business, then the deduction is up to 20% of business income, but subject to a limitation based on wages or depreciable property in service that also phases in such that the limit fully applies at taxable income of $213,300 ($426,600 MFJ). The wage limitation when fully phased in applies such that the most you can deduct is the greater of 50% of W-2 wages paid by the company (including your own wages) or 25% of W-2 wages plus 2.5% of the original basis of all qualified property***

This is an over-simplified explanation and I don't want to overcomplicate this in a Tax Update Book, but every year a few more winkles seem to surface. They mainly involve how you aggregate multiple businesses, how certain expenses and taxes affect the final number, and how losses are accounted for. The first two are mainly handled by software, and don't affect things too significantly, but the third matters. Basically, it doesn't make sense if you had massive losses in a prior year to ignore those and get the 20% deduction on a subsequent profitable year. This didn't come into play in the first year, but now, if you had losses in 2018, you can't take the deduction in 2019 until the profits in 2019 exceed the losses from 2018. They call these "carryovers" which I think is confusing because there are tons of other carryover losses in the tax world, but that's what they gave us to work with.

*This rule is very unusual in that you need to do your tax return all the way through to the point of just before figuring out your tax amount, and THEN apply this deduction. It uses taxable income for virtually all tests and calculations, as opposed to Gross or Adjusted Gross Income like almost everything else in the tax world.

**From the bill, "A specified service trade or business means any trade or business involving the performance of services in the fields of health, law, consulting, athletics, financial services, brokerage services, or any trade or business where the principal asset of such trade or business is the reputation or skill of one or more of its employees or owners, or which involves the performance of services that consist of investing and investment management trading, or dealing in securities, partnership interests, or commodities." Architects and engineers are specifically noted as NOT subject to this limitation. There are a lot of specific business lists available online to help you sort this out.

***From the Bill: "qualified property means tangible property of a character subject to depreciation that is held by, and available for use in, the qualified trade or business at the close of the taxable year, and which is used in the production of qualified business income, and for which the depreciable period has not ended before the close of the taxable year. The depreciable period with respect to qualified property of a taxpayer means the period beginning on the date the property is first placed in service by the taxpayer and ending on the later of (a) the date 10 years after that date, or (b) the last day of the last full year in the applicable recovery period that would apply to the property under section 168 (without regard to section 168(g))."

## My Advice:

1. Use a good professional for this or be very careful about how your software handles it, especially if you are in the income phaseout ranges or have losses in some years.
2. It is absolutely critical that you make sure to account for information from previous tax years, especially losses, when filing tax returns for later years. If you use the same software or preparer

every year, it will generally carry things forward properly. If you do not, make sure that you exercise great care in finding the appropriate information from a prior year tax return to carry into your current year. This is not the only tax item that can be messed up when switching software or preparers. Good preparers know which questions to ask and how to handle it. Software might not.

# How Does This Stuff Affect My Business?

The Trump Tax Law had lots of changes, the biggest of which is the new 20% deduction for "pass-through" entities. You should have just read a whole chapter on that, so I'm not going to rehash it here. Same with the reduction of the corporate tax rate to 21%.

Here is a list of other changes:

The limit on deductions for state and local taxes does not apply to businesses. There has been no change to the deductibility of state and local taxes by businesses.

They extended bonus depreciation for another few years, through 2026. They also expanded the amount of section 179 deduction you can take in a year to $1,000,000 and expanded what items qualify. Both changes will allow you to deduct more money from capital expenditures in the year you make them.

For 2020 the section 179 deduction limit is $1,040,000.

More businesses qualify to use the cash method of accounting:

They eliminated the ability to carryback Net Operating Losses, they must now be carried forward to future years, however the Coronavirus bills reversed this for a few years, allowing you to carryback 2018, 2019 and 2020 losses, essentially granting a possibly retroactive deduction that could put money in your pocket immediately by amending prior year's taxes…though since the IRS was not opening their mail at the time of this writing, they won't be looking at amendments.

Almost all entertainment expenses, other than meals for employees (or facilities for them) have been made non-deductible:

The Coronavirus Bill fixed what was called the "Retail Glitch" on depreciation of Qualified Improvement Property. Basically, the law intended for you to be able to immediately deduct this kind of expense but failed to properly define it as 15-year property, so it didn't work. This was fixed retroactively to 2017.

Social Security Taxes can be deferred for 2020. They must be repaid in 2021 and 2022, half in each year by the last day of the year. Self-employed people can take advantage of this deferment for 6.2% of their self-employment taxes (the employer's portion of the Social Security component).

You can get a credit for days the Coronavirus made you unable to work. There was a previous chapter with details on the subject.

If you got a Paycheck Protection Program Loan, you may deduct normally deductible items you used the money for even if the loan is forgiven.

For 2021 and 2022 100% of business meals may be deducted vice just 50%

There are many more obscure changes that most people would not understand and that are pretty complicated, especially involving foreign investment and income. I am not going to bury you with those here.

**My Advice:**

1. If you had Net Operating Losses in 2018 or 2019, look into carrying them back. A professional can help a lot with this.
2. If you have a complicated business entity, employees or think any of the weirder provisions discussed here apply to you, seek a professional to help you manage them.
3. Work with a tax professional to decide if it is wise to take advantage of the Social Security deferment.

# Inflation Adjustment Changes

There are many provisions of tax law that are "inflation adjusted". This basically means that they go up as the cost of living goes up. The Trump Tax Law changed how this is calculated, in a way that is not favorable to taxpayers, but is minor initially (though the effect will be magnified as it is compounded over years). They used to use the Consumer Price Index, but now will use something called the Chained Consumer Price Index.

Explanations for this are way too wonky to include here, except to mention that it means tax benefits will be muted going forward, due to things like tax brackets and deductions going up more slowly over time than they would otherwise.

I have no specific advice for you here, it is just information.

# States That Start with Taxable Income

One of the under-appreciated aspects of Trump Tax Law is how it will affect the few states that start their tax calculation with Federal Taxable Income.

Most states start with Adjusted Gross Income, which is calculated BEFORE standard/itemized deductions and exemptions. Some start with Gross Income, which is before EVERY deduction, some use their own system entirely, and a very few start with Taxable Income.

Most states will see some effect transferred from the Federal changes to their return, but the changes to the standard deductions and exemptions mean these will be exaggerated in states that start with Taxable Income. If you live in one of these states, watch for law changes to account for this, or expect your state tax return to improve or degrade along with the Federal.

The few remaining states that (as best I could tell at time of publishing) start with Taxable Income are:

Colorado
Minnesota
North Dakota
South Carolina

Many states have been tweaking their laws to account for expected effects on their tax receipts. These are too numerous to discuss here, except to note that Vermont has decoupled from taxable income and that most tax schemes by high tax states to turn their taxes into charitable deductions to evade the State Tax deduction limit were squashed by the IRS.

## My Advice:

1. If you are from one of the states that start with taxable income, keep an eye on your state website to see if they make major changes. Also recognize that in those states, anything that provides a

deduction on the Federal side has (usually) a corresponding positive effect on the state side.

2. Having a good working knowledge of how your state converts your Federal tax information into a State tax return can be very useful in ensuring your software doesn't mess up your taxes or miss out on some deductions. I always recommend reading your state's form instructions every year. A lot of times there are cool things you can do to lower your taxes.

# Working from Home or Tele-Commuting

If you did not already figure it out, you're getting hosed. At least from a steady state to steady state perspective – you are losing deductions and not getting much back. The elimination of the employee business expenses essentially prevents you from deducting any of the costs of working from home.

The original 2% of AGI floor on these deductions prevented a lot of people from taking advantage of this, and the increase in the standard deduction will take some of the sting out of it, but for some people this might really hurt.

You are going to have to decide if working from home is still worth it, or if you can negotiate an increase in salary from your employer. Keep in mind that the salary increase will probably all be taxable, but more money is more money. You can also consider trying to get your employer to pay for some of the things that you would normally pay for when working from home.

Once you file your 2018 and 2019 tax returns, you should have a much better idea how this affected you and have additional ammunition for negotiations with your employer. Make sure you discuss this with your tax professional or take a careful look at your return if you prepare it yourself.

Anecdotally, it doesn't look like most employers are stepping up to help out their employees on this, at least among my clients. I do not know if it's changing what happens with new hires.

One way to ensure you don't bear employment expenses out of pocket is for your employer to reimburse them under an "accountable plan". This makes the payments tax-free to you, and deductible by your employer. An accountable plan simply means they pay you in advance or reimburse you for actual expenses, properly accounting for them within 60 days to ensure you receive reimbursement for things you paid for or pay back any excess advances. There's some slop to the 60 days, but your employer needs to figure out their plan's timeframes and make sure it complies with the rules. Most things require an exact dollar for dollar amount, but they can reimburse you a standard mileage rate as well as a federally established daily meal rate.

**A Coronavirus Comment**: As discussed earlier, this change has particular application during the COVID-19 Pandemic. Before this change, working from home could result in a number of deductions for home office, travel, supplies, ZOOM subscriptions and many other things. NONE of these are deductible for an employee, even if COVID has forced them to work from home. A self-employed person might be able to deduct all of these things, but the Trump Tax Law eliminated ALL employee business deductions.

## My Advice:

1. Try to get your employer to create an accountable plan as discussed above.
2. When starting a new job, be sure to discuss what expenses will be reimbursed and if they will have an accountable plan for them. Take this into account when negotiating salary. Recognize that there are positive aspects of working from home, mainly saving on commuting costs and hassles. Working from home is probably a net plus compared to going to work, but people who are used to having a deduction that they have now last feel it the most.

# Driving and Travelling for Work (esp Sales)

This chapter is basically the same as the last chapter, except to emphasize that mileage was probably a HUGE deduction for you, and negotiations discussed below (in the cut and paste from the previous chapter) should include talk of a company car or mileage reimbursement. If you are a kick ass salesman, you should be able to make this work.

Truckers paid on a W-2 are going to be hard hit in this area, so be prepared to talk to your employer.

Begin (mostly) cut and paste section:

If you didn't already figure it out, you're getting hosed. The elimination of the employee business expenses essentially prevents you from deducting any of the costs of working from home.

The original 2% of AGI floor on these deductions prevented a lot of people from taking advantage of this, and the increase in the standard deduction will take some of the sting out of it, but for some people this might really hurt.

You are going to have to decide if this kind of work is still worth it, or if you can negotiate an increase in salary from your employer, shift to an accountable plan, or become a 1099 contractor (making everything deductible again but also making you responsible for ALL your taxes). Keep in mind that the salary increase will probably all be taxable, but more money is more money. You can also consider trying to get your employer to pay for some of the things that you would normally pay for when working from home.

Once you file your 2018 and 2019 tax returns, you should have a much better idea how this affected you and have additional ammunition for negotiations with your employer. Make sure you discuss this with your tax professional or take a careful look at your return if you prepare it yourself.

Anecdotally, it doesn't look like most employers are stepping up to help out their employees on this, at least among my clients. I do not know if it is changing what happens with new hires.

One way to ensure you do not bear employment expenses out of pocket is for your employer to reimburse them under an "accountable plan". This makes the payments tax-free to you, and deductible by your employer. An accountable plan simply means they pay you in advance or reimburse you for actual expenses, properly accounting for them within 60 days to ensure you receive reimbursement for things you paid for or pay back any excess advances. There's some slop to the 60 days, but your employer needs to figure out their plan's timeframes and make sure it complies with the rules. Most things require an exact dollar for dollar amount, but they can reimburse you a standard mileage rate as well as a federally established daily meal rate.

**My Advice:**

1. Try to get your employer to create an accountable plan as discussed above.
2. When starting a new job, be sure to discuss what expenses will be reimbursed and if they will have an accountable plan for them. Take this into account when negotiating salary.
3. Consider shifting to be a 1099 paid contractor. Recognize that this has HUGE implications for taxes, and requires advice from a professional, but the higher your expenses are as a percentage of your income, the more this makes sense.

# Is my Rental Property Affected?

Maybe. But probably not. If it is, probably in a good way.

The change in deductibility of mortgage interest and real estate taxes does not affect your rental property. Changes in depreciation rules also make very little difference here.

It looks like the new 20% deduction for business income in the Trump Tax Law MIGHT apply to you, but probably not. That, plus the fact that most rentals operate at a taxable loss, means that you will probably see zero effect on your rental property with regard to taxes.

As far as rental property is concerned, it will be a "facts and circumstances" determination. If it is a business, based on "facts and circumstances" then it will be eligible for the deduction. Obviously, someone renting a former house out using a property manager probably won't qualify, but the more time spent on rentals, and the more businesslike it is run, the more likely it is to be eligible. Since most rentals start out at a loss, and these losses must be accounted for before eligible for the deduction, it seems most small landlords will find it more trouble than it's worth. That said, a decision needs to be made early how to try to handle this (though it can change as circumstances do) and professional help is probably warranted when deciding. This is a BIG complicated situation, with long-term implications, so paying for help early can be worth its weight in gold (or fees).

The IRS has established "Safe Harbor" rules to allow you to use the deduction for rental properties without worrying about your circumstances being disputed. They require that you perform 250 hours per year on "rental services". This is pretty hard to meet for a single rental. Services include maintenance, cleaning, rent collection, paperwork, legal efforts, advertising, finding tenants and pretty much anything else involved in managing the property. Efforts to find new property, and related efforts such as gathering or arranging financing, do not count. You must maintain separate records for the rental and they must be "contemporaneous" meaning you maintain them in real time, vice reconstructing at a later date. If the rental has been in existence for more than four years, you only have to meet the test in three of the prior five years including the year in question.

If you have a not for profit rental, where you were deducting expenses on Schedule A instead of Schedule E, you can no longer deduct expenses, but you still have to claim the income.

For perspective, the following is copied from my major tax book: Everyday Taxes. It includes pretty much everything you need to know about rentals:

This section is designed for the average homeowner who is converting their personal residence into rental property, either because they are unable to sell it, intend to reside in it later, or simply hope to use it as an investment. It does not cover all the specifics of how to file a Rental Property tax return; rather, it covers record keeping and tax issues that an owner of Residential Rental Real Estate should be aware of. This section does not discuss Alternative Minimum Tax implications of Rental Property. I feel strongly that you should have a tax pro help you, at least for the first year, and have any self-prepared tax returns checked once in a while.

## When does it become Rental Property?

It is rental property the day it is available for rent. This is when you can start deducting expenses. Generally, when you put the sign out front, put the ad in the paper, or tell your co-workers to find you a tenant, you have made it available for rent.

## What is Rent?

Rent is the full amount of rent received. If you have a property manager who deducts a commission, the rent is the full rent paid (including the commission) and the commission is a deduction. Similarly, if your tenant performs a repair and deducts the cost from the rent, the rent is the full amount of the rent and the deducted amount is a repair expense. If someone pays advance rent, include it in the year received. If a security deposit is paid, it becomes rent when you keep it to cover an expense (and the expense becomes a deduction). If the deposit is agreed as non-refundable (such as a pet cleaning deposit) it is rent when received. If the tenant is supposed to pay rent and doesn't, do not include the amount not paid as rent. This means there is no "bad debt" deduction for rental—if you don't get it, it's not rent.

## Deductible Expenses:

You can deduct all reasonable and necessary expenses for the rental of your home. Some items must be depreciated over their useful life (defined by the IRS). Be careful and make sure to do this right—there's more information coming later in the section. These must be expenses you pay for—your labor is not an expense. Here is a fairly comprehensive list of expenses:

Mortgage interest (pro-rate by day for the first year of rental)
Taxes (pro-rate by day for the first year of rental)
Insurance (pro-rate by day for the first year of rental)
Mortgage insurance premiums (pro-rate by day for the first year of rental)
Homeowner's association dues
Pest control
Utilities you pay (including those paid when unoccupied but available for rent)
Advertising expenses
Repairs
Landscaping
Painting
Legal expenses for collecting rent, preparing leases, evicting tenants
Improvements
Tax prep fees for rental-related forms
Management fees
Cleaning expenses
Travel and mileage to manage the rental property (the primary purpose of the trip must be to manage the rental property—don't try to deduct a vacation during which you "check on" the rental.)

Starting in 2018, there's a new deduction called the Qualified Business Income Deduction which can apply to rental property if all facts and circumstances indicate that you treat it like a business. There is a safe harbor rule that you can use to ensure the IRS will accept the deduction, but it is difficult to meet if you are only renting out one former home. The starting point for the Safe Harbor is that you spend 250 hours of rental services for the rental during the year. You must also maintain separate income and expense books for the rental and maintain contemporaneous (made as the events occur – not recreated) records of the services you provide and the hours you spend on them to support the Safe Harbor time requirements.

If you qualify for the deduction, you get to deduct 20% of your profit off of your taxable income. If you make less than $326,600 taxable income on your tax return (for Married Filing Jointly - $163,300 for everyone else*) it's as simple as that. Actually, it's not simple at all, especially if you exceed the income limits we just discussed, but your tax pro or software should be able to handle it. If you make more than the limit above, your deduction will phase out unless you pay wages (or have a lot of equipment). I've already covered this in a previous chapter, so I'm not rehashing it here.

*The MFS limit is actually $25 higher based on my reading of the new limits, which seems like a mistake – so I'll be looking into the reason for the slight difference.

Make very certain to save receipts for all of these and report the amounts to your tax preparer. A ledger where you write the date, a descriptions and the amount of an expense can be very helpful to not miss things.

**Depreciation:**

Depreciation is how you deduct the cost of major items with a life longer than 1 year. You will deduct a portion of the cost a little at a time over a specified number of years. Do not let someone tell you not to depreciate so you can avoid recapture—you have to recapture any depreciation allowed (whether deducted or not). Failing to depreciate rental property is one of the most common mistakes made by self-preparers, and it is a BIG one.

You will depreciate the building, appliances and any improvements to the property, as well as certain landscaping items (fences, trees, etc.). It is important to understand that if you have a major expense that increases the value, or prolongs the life of your property, it will likely be depreciated vice deducted. Repairs that do not increase the value or extend the life may be deducted. Examples of improvements are air conditioner replacement, roof replacement, adding a fence or patio, and making additions to the structure. Examples of repairs are painting, replacing garbage disposal, repairing a hole in the roof without replacing it, repairing the air conditioner unit.

When converting your home to rental you need to know the Basis. This is generally the price you paid for the home, plus any improvements you made to it (see IRS Pub 551, or a tax professional for other things that might affect it). If the Fair Market Value (FMV) the day you convert it to rental property is less than this value, then this is your basis. The FMV is what your house would sell for to a willing buyer. You also need to know what the land is worth. You subtract this from the basis before depreciating the basis. You can determine the land value from your property tax card or by comparing to other similar properties sold in the area. You will depreciate the house by taking an even portion of the basis every month for the next 27.5 years (this means the first year's deduction will be smaller, and the deduction for the rest of the years will be about the same). Your tax pro will need the basis, land price, FMV, date purchased and date available for rent for your house.

Improvements are depreciated for 27.5 years just like the house. Appliances are depreciated for 5 years and landscaping improvements are depreciated for 15 years. See IRS Pub 527 for how to depreciate 5- and 15-year property. Your tax preparer will need to know the date you bought these items and the price you paid for them (including installation if you paid for it). Recent changes to depreciation rules created a "Safe Harbor" that allows you not to depreciate (meaning you can deduct it immediately) any individual purchase or improvement that is less than $2,500. You have to maintain certain records in order to do this, so ask for help if this applies to you.

## Do I need a Property Manager?

I like property managers. They will keep about 10% of your rent, but if they can save you 1 month of vacancy, they have paid for 10 months of commissions. If you try to rent without one, and can generally keep the place occupied, you probably are okay without one. If you try to rent it and it goes more than a month empty, get referrals and hire a property manager. Similarly, if you have a property manager and your house goes vacant more than a month, find a new property manager.

## Active Participation:

It generally behooves you to be an active participant in the renting of your property. You can be an active participant even if you have a property manager. If you make the decisions about what rent to charge, what repairs to make, and whether to allow pets, you are actively participating. Even if the manager says: "I think we should raise the rent to $1,200." and you have to give the OK, you are actively participating. By being an active participant, you can generally deduct up to $25,000 of rental loss from the rest of your income (subject to income and filing status limitations). If you are totally passive in the rental, you cannot deduct any losses. If you are passive, or you have losses in excess of the limit, you will have to carry them over until you have a gain or dispose of the property. The income limits kick in at $100,000 of AGI and the loss is not deductible above $150,000 AGI.

## At Risk Issues:

You may be asked if you are "At Risk" for the full amount of your rental. This means that you are not protected from losses on the property should everything go south on you. Generally speaking, unless you have some sort of a loan that you would not have to pay back (such as from a family member) you are At Risk for the full amount.

## Tax Implications When Selling:

When selling a house that has been used as rental property, it is generally treated as a sale of a business asset. Thus, it is a fully taxable transaction. It will be reported on Form 4797 (Sale of Business Assets). The form will ask for the date purchased, date sold, the sale price (minus expenses of sale) and the Basis. Other than basis, these entries are fairly self-explanatory. The basis is that which you are using to depreciate the home. It is the price paid (or FMV when converted to rental if this was lower than the basis) + the cost of any improvements – any depreciation taken or allowed. There are other things that might affect the basis, but they are unusual and won't normally be seen. The gain or loss is the difference between the basis and the sales price.

It is possible to still use the exclusion for the Sale of Main Home if you meet the requirements. This will normally only occur if you lived in the home for at least two years before you rented it out and sold it within three years of renting it. If this is the case, you may be able to exclude up to $250,000 of the gain ($500,000 if MFJ). You may use this exclusion for all gain, except that attributable to depreciation.

## Personal Use or Part-Year Rentals:

If you rent your property for only part of the year, or you rent only a portion of your property (such as a room or a duplex) you need to pro-rate your expenses. Your tax pro will need to know the status of the property for each day of the year (rented, occupied by you, occupied by family, vacant, vacant but available for rent). They will also need to know the square footage of the property that is rental use, personal use and communal use, as well as which expenses cover the whole property (mortgage, taxes, etc.) and which are exclusive to the rental portion (repairs to that portion, utilities billed separately, etc.). There are more intricacies of this—contact your tax pro for more details.

**State Issues:**

If you rent out a property in a state that is not your state of residency, make sure you make this clear to your tax pro and make sure you understand how each state handles it. South Carolina, for example, requires you to add an out-of-state rental loss back and subtract an out-of-state rental gain from income.

**A Coronavirus Comment**: If you lost rental income during Coronavirus, there is no specific tax change to help you, but, if you don't get the rent, you don't include it in income, so you get a "deduction" for lost rent. That said, when they pay the back rent, it will increase your income in the later year, so be prepared for this.

**My Advice:**

1. Keep good records for your rental. Have a file where you keep receipts and maintain a record of income and expenses. If a property manager handles an expense, make sure they provide a detailed report at the end of the year. Also keep records substantiating the date it is available for rent, as well as how you determined your basis. Taking the original closing folder you got when you bought it and adding documentation of improvement expenses is a good idea. Keeping a log sheet with dates, descriptions and costs will also help a lot in the future.
2. Use a tax professional in the first year you rent the property and in the year you sell it, at a minimum. Mistakes made in the first year of rental property taxes can haunt you for a long time, and have HUGE implications when you sell.
3. Depreciate your rental property. You have to recapture depreciation that is allowed, even if you don't deduct it. This is one of the biggest mistakes people make!
4. Do not deduct rental expenses as itemized deductions. I am still stunned how often I see mortgage interest for a rental deducted on BOTH schedule A (Itemized deductions) and Schedule E (Rental Property).
5. Pay attention to the date you lose your personal residence exclusion. This is generally three years from the date you moved out (13 years for military as long as you remain on active duty). As this

date approaches, if the property has gone up significantly in value, selling it and avoiding taxes on the gain can be a big deal.

Remember that you still have to pay taxes on depreciation taken or allowed, so it is not a get out of taxes free card.

6. If you only have one or two rentals, chasing the 20% deduction is probably not worth it, and be wary of a tax professional that uses it without discussing the required documentation.

7. If you think you might qualify, or you want to be certain, start keeping active and separate records of your expenses AND the time you perform rental services as discussed above. If you hit the 250-hour threshold (combined if you have multiple rentals) then you can have the 20% deduction IF the rentals are profitable.

# Alimony

In the past, alimony paid was deducted by the person paying it, and included as income by the person receiving it. This has been eliminated starting in 2019.

**Affecting 2019 and later**: Obviously, Congress recognized that people were actively negotiating divorces that would take effect in 2018, so they delayed this part of the law until 2019. This only applies to NEW divorce agreements. If you are already paying alimony, nothing has changed. Starting with 2019 settlements, the payment of alimony is a tax neutral event (nobody deducts it and nobody includes it as income).

If you end up negotiating a divorce that will be signed in 2019, make sure you take these changes into account.

The IRS has established rules for changes to existing divorce decrees. Generally, a change to a divorce decree will have no effect on the deductibility of alimony, even if it is executed in 2019 or later. If it was executed in 2018 or before, alimony continues to be deductible by the payer and is income to the recipient. The only way this changes on a renegotiated decree is if it both changes the alimony provisions AND specifically states that the alimony will no longer be treated as income by the recipient and be deductible by the payer.

## My Advice:

1. Do not assume your lawyer knows about these rules. For a new divorce, make sure you negotiate based on the fact that (as the payer of alimony) you are still stuck paying the taxes on money you send off, or (as the recipient) you get the income tax free. For a renegotiated divorce, make sure your lawyer understands that it is possible to change the deductibility/taxability of alimony if the decree is executed correctly.
2. In the very rare situation that the recipient of alimony is in a higher tax bracket than the payer, this is an opportunity to renegotiate the alimony and change it to a non-taxable transfer. This

allows both parties to win by lowering the overall amount of alimony, while increasing the after-tax income of the recipient. A good tax pro and lawyer working together can calculate the most beneficial way to handle this.

3. On a non-tax change aside, most tax lawyers think they can change tax law with a divorce decree. They cannot. Except in very specific circumstances as allowed by tax law, a child must live with you more than half the year for you to claim most child tax benefits. No divorce decree can change this. You cannot be Head of Household if you do not have a child living with you more than half the year, even if your decree says you get to claim the child. Talk to a tax professional BEFORE you negotiate your divorce!

# Moving Expenses Are No Longer Deductible

If you moved for work, you used to be able to deduct a lot of things you had to pay for the move. If your employer paid them, you did not have to pay taxes on that money. Now, under Trump Tax, you cannot deduct ANYTHING for moving. If your employer reimburses you, or pays moving expenses for you, you have to pay taxes on that money as if they paid it for work. (This is over-simplified, so talk to a professional or your Human Resources if you have moving expenses paid or reimbursed by your employer).

Many companies used to pay you extra to cover taxes on reimbursements that were not deductible or excludable (like house buying assistance). Employees should be looking to negotiate these extra payments for entire moves if they have leverage.

This change does not apply to active duty military moving on Permanent Change of Station Orders.

**My Advice:**

1. If you are getting reimbursed for a move, make sure you understand if they are paying extra to cover the taxes. They would pay this directly to the IRS and states as withholding. If they are NOT doing this, you can find yourself in real tax trouble at the end of the year since this income has no withholding. Increase your withholding or save money to cover the taxes. A move year is also a good year to go nuts with Goodwill type donations, offloading all the crap you have so you don't have to move it and getting a potential deduction in the process. All of this in a year with a potentially higher tax bracket making the deductions more valuable.

2. Use the IRS Tax Withholding Estimator discussed previously after you get your first few post-move paychecks to see exactly where you sit and adjust according to the advice it provides.

# Estate Taxes

The exemption was effectively doubled, but in a weird way. It was made $10,000,000, but indexed for inflation from back in 2010, so the exemption calculates out to $11,200,000 in 2018, and will go up from there until it reverts back to $5,000,000 on January 1$^{st}$, 2026 (unless action is taken.)

This means that the estate of someone who dies in 2018 can exclude $11,200,000 from estate taxes. That number goes up for every year after 2018 until 2026, when it drops back down.

The exclusion for 2020 is $11,580,000

## My Advice:

1. It is generally not a good idea to plan your date of death around Estate Tax Rates and Exclusions.
2. Too many people put too much work and money into estate planning that is not necessary. If you are below the above thresholds, making sure you have designated beneficiaries for all of your money and retirement accounts, have updated life insurance beneficiaries, have a will, and provide easy to find instructions on where all your money and stuff is will usually make your passing easier on your heirs without a lot of unneeded expense or effort.

# Changes to the Alternative Minimum Tax

I am not going to go into a ton of detail here, mainly because the Alternative Minimum Tax is a completely different tax system from the income tax we are used to, and very few people are affected by it. The AMT is a neat trick that the government came up with a number of years ago to make sure that even the super-rich, with tons of deductions, paid their fair share. It now affects millions of people and can be quite disturbing if you are subject to it. Early in my career as a Tax Super Genius, I would be working on tax returns and find that the refund stopped changing, even though there was plenty of room for deductions, and I kept adding them in. I soon learned this was the AMT at work.

The AMT basically gives you very few deductions but has a very large standard deduction (called an exemption for AMT). The exemption was designed to get smaller once you reached a certain higher income. It has only two tax rates, 26% and 28%. You generally get sucked into this if you have a large income, and/or lots of deductions. The Trump Tax Law made the exemption significantly larger and the income at which it starts getting smaller, so fewer people will face AMT. These are pre and post 2018 numbers for comparison (2020 numbers are at the end of this chapter): From $84,500 Married Filing Joint (MFJ), $54,300 Single (S) or Head of Household (HH) and $42,250 Married Filing Separately (MFS) to $109,400 MFJ, $70,300 S or HH and $54,700 MFS. These are some pretty nice new numbers.

They also raise the point at which the exemption starts dropping to $1,000,000 MFJ and $500,000 for all other filing statuses. For perspective, the old value was $160,900 for MFJ. This is also a big deal.

To make things more confusing, the tax forms do not have a separate return where you calculate AMT and then compare it to your regular tax. What they do have is a short form (Form 6251) that essentially undoes everything not allowed in AMT, and then adds in the stuff that's allowed. It then compares your AMT tax to regular tax, and if the AMT is higher, adds the difference to your regular tax. This makes it very difficult to really understand what's happening to your return because of AMT and makes it hard to strategize to minimize taxes.

If, when you are reviewing your tax return, there is a number on Form 1040 Schedule 2, Line 45, you have been hit with AMT. You should consider talking to a professional to see if there's anything you can do, and to develop strategies for future years to minimize it. There is a recapture provision that allows you to get back some AMT you paid in prior years, but it too, is amazingly complicated.

The exemptions are $113,400 MFJ and $72,900 Single or HH for 2020.

**My Advice:**

1. Charitable deductions are one of the few rock-solid ways to minimize AMT.

# The Penalty for Not Having Insurance is Gone

This has been eliminated. Starting in 2019 the shared responsibility payment, and all its exceptions have been eliminated, but not until 2019.

To be clear, we are talking about the Affordable Care Act's penalty, of up to 2.5% of your income that is imposed for not having health insurance.

There is a potential court case that might make this go away retroactively. It is too late to get a penalty in 2016 back if the case wins, but 2017 and 2018 are on the table.

Here is the rub: The statute of limitations for claiming a refund for 2017 expires in April of 2021 and we don't know if the case will be resolved by then!

So, what do you do? You file a "Protective Claim" for a refund. You should do this for all years you paid the penalty, not just 2017. In Publication 17, the IRS describes how to do this:

"Generally, a protective claim is a formal claim or amended return for credit or refund normally based on current litigation or expected changes in tax law or other legislation. You file a protective claim when your right to a refund is contingent on future events and may not be determinable until after the statute of limitations expires. A valid protective claim doesn't have to list a particular dollar amount or demand an immediate refund. However, a valid protective claim must:
Be in writing and signed;
Include your name, address, SSN or ITIN, and other contact information;
Identify and describe the contingencies affecting the claim;
Clearly alert the IRS to the essential nature of the claim; and
Identify the specific year(s) for which a refund is sought.
Mail your protective claim for refund to the address listed in the Instructions for Form 1040X under *Where To File*. Generally, the

IRS will delay action on the protective claim until the contingency is resolved."

Basically, file an amended return (1040X) and write at the top of the front page: "Filing a Protective Claim for ACA penalty refund per Texas vs. U.S., No. 19-10011 (5th Cir. December 18, 2019)" Mail to the address in the Amended return instructions. Then wait...and wait...If the court case is upheld all the way to the Supreme Court - REFUND!

# The Kiddie Tax is Easier Now

Everything discussed below was changed RETROACTIVELY back to its original form. This means that if you paid the new higher rates discussed below, you can go back and use the old rates by amending your tax returns for 2018 and/or 2019.

Here is the Trump Tax Change with discussion of what Kiddie Tax is: The "Kiddie Tax" was one of the most irritating aspects of tax law before this new tax bill. It was designed to prevent parents from transferring investments to their kids to avoid paying a fair rate of taxes on it. The way they did this was annoying, complicated and stupid. Essentially, if your child had more than $2100 of investment income (though they included all unearned income, even unemployment) the taxes were paid at the rate it would have been had it been on the parent's tax return. Needless to say, this was a mess. Parents could also include it on their return as if it was their income.

The kiddie tax applied to kids until they turned 18, or up to 24 if they did not provide over half their own support. This has not been changed.

The new law basically eliminates the kiddie tax, and taxes investment income of children as if it was in a trust/estate. This taxes it at a higher rate than if it was just the kid's income, but not at a variable rate based on their parents.

Form 8615 will be used to calculate the taxes on the child's return. The tax rates go as high as 37%. Below is a link to the 2018 Form Instructions, which has the tax rates on the first page:

https://www.irs.gov/pub/irs-pdf/i8615.pdf

Again, to be clear, in December of 2019, everything just discussed disappeared and Kiddie Tax now works the way it always has.

**My Advice**: If you paid Kiddie Tax in 2018 or 2019, amend your or your child's tax return to apply the lower tax rates. It will be complicated, because the old rules were a mess, potentially combining information from both the parent's and the child's tax return, but the tax was way lower.

# Head of Household Issues

Most people will probably not notice what they did with Head of Household on the Trump Tax Bill, but it actually matters. They did not change the numbers or requirements. What they did, is make it more important not to cheat in this area.

Some background (my personal interpretation of motivations is included and could be wrong): A couple years ago, Congress figured out (or finally acknowledged) how much fraud there was involved in refundable credits like the Earned Income Credit, Additional Child Tax Credit and the American Opportunity Credit. To combat this, they tightened the rules on documentation and reporting, AND they added a due diligence requirement on tax professionals. For all intents and purposes, I am allowed to believe my clients when they tell me something, even if it seems weird or far-fetched. For those credits I just mentioned, they changed that and require me to ask and document additional questions if information provided does not add up or seems inconsistent. I also have to inform my clients of the importance of being honest and the repercussions of failing to be.

This should give you the idea that they are paying close attention to these areas, and the number of letters I have seen regarding the American Opportunity Credit in particular bear this out.

The Trump Tax Law extended these requirements to claiming Head of Household starting in 2019. So, make sure you know the rules and follow them (see the earlier chapter on Filing Status).

**My Advice**: Do not cheat on this. It is usually very obvious when you qualify for Head of Household. If it is not obvious, be careful and/or ask for professional advice.

# A Couple of Things for the Military

**Military Spouses Residency Relief Act**: I want to simplify the MSRRA for most active duty personnel. States have taken this incredibly simple Act, and made it sound about as complicated as it can be. I expect they are also going to fight to twist its words to try to maximize their tax revenues.

The spouse of a military member has two choices for state of residency: the state they are physically residing in, or the active military service member's state. For 2017 and before, in order to claim the service member's state, they have to have previously established residency in that state, usually by living there and doing the usual resident things (driver's license, job, home, registering to vote, etc.) It should be easy to determine if you qualify for this choice, with one little exception...

Applying common sense, this decision should normally be made at the time the spouse first marries the service member, or when one half of the already married couple joins the military. In this case, it is simple and easy. The fact that the military couple buys a home, has kids, lives for an extended period of time in the new state should have no impact on this election (assuming the spouse doesn't register to vote or take other positive action to indicate they want to become a resident of the state they're stationed in.) Where this becomes interesting is when a couple stays in the military for many years, over many duty stations. Most states will have issues if you (the spouse) change your state of residency back and forth based on the relative tax advantages of the various states you move between over the course of a career. They would assume that once you make your election, that is it. I could make arguments either way, but, be aware that if you keep changing states, you might have to fight over it.

In direct contradiction to what I wrote above, in 2018, the law was modified and changed the requirement that the spouse establish residency in the military member's state. It also appeared to greatly relax the restrictions on changing states of residency by the spouse. Basically, starting in 2018 and later, a spouse can choose to be a resident of the state they live in, or the military member's state, and it would seem they can change it back and forth from duty station to duty station. I doubt the states see it like that, but the law is pretty clear. You really don't have to worry about driver's license and cars being registered in the state you live in – most states prefer or require you to do those things and it doesn't change how the MSRRA applies. Always register to vote in the state you want as your residence.

Make sure you understand exactly where each state stands with regard to taxation before making your decision, since the state you decide to be a resident of will expect you to file a tax return and pay taxes, even though you work in the state you are stationed in. Just because Ohio does not tax the active military member's income does not mean the spouse gets off scot-free. The MSRRA is not a get out of taxes free card for military spouses.

**Moving Expenses**: Remember that moving expenses were eliminated with the Trump Tax Law, EXCEPT for military Permanent Change of Station moves. This includes the move upon discharge or retirement. Generally this would only apply to a Do It Yourself (DITY) move, where you move and get reimbursed. The reimbursement will be on a separate W-2, found under Travel/Misc W-2 on MyPay. A non DITY move might have a few deductible expenses, such as the cost of shipping a second car or a pet (but not quarantine or medical preparations for them), since these are often not reimbursed by the military.

**Reserve Travel**: If you travel more than 100 miles for training, you can deduct unreimbursed expenses for this travel. Lodging, mileage, air fares, meals, and rental cars are all deductible (not meals if you have access to messing facilities). These are deductible as employee business expenses on Form 2106 even though the Trump Tax Law eliminated them for everyone else. They also may be deducted without needing to itemize.

Reserve members called to active duty get a myriad of benefits and exclusions too numerous to list here. One commonly missed one is that if you are called to active duty for more than 180 days, early retirement withdrawals are not subject to the extra 10% penalty (this does not change the fact that early retirement withdrawals are a bad idea).

**The Payroll Tax Holiday**: You should be receiving detailed and very specific training on how this is going to affect you in 2021. ABSOLUTELY make sure you are prepared for the pay reduction you have coming.

**My Advice:**

1. Talk to a tax professional or do serious research into the specifics of state taxation for the state you are stationed in, and your military state of residence before deciding to take advantage of the MSRRA.
2. If you get stationed in a state with no income tax, file DD Form 2058 with your Personnel Department to change your state of residency to that state so you and your spouse will never pay state taxes again (while in the military).
3. Most jobs will automatically withhold state taxes even when you qualify to not be a resident and some states make it a pain to get the money back. Every state has a method to avoid state taxes being withheld, so you need to aggressively pursue that when you start a job.
4. Make sure you check for the extra W-2 if you do a DITY move. It will be received in the year you received the reimbursement, so it is possible to have a deduction in one year and income in another year.

# Some Cancelled Student Loans Are Not Taxable

To be honest, this is not so much a change as a clarification of where things were probably headed anyway.

A lot of people don't realize that when someone cancels debt that you owe, you often have to pay taxes on the cancelled debt as income. This is true of student loans. There are ways around it, mostly by using the insolvency exclusion to avoid claiming cancelled student loans as income.

The Trump Tax Law made clear that if your loan is cancelled due to death or permanent and total disability, that the cancelled debt does not count as income. The IRS defines total and permanent disability different than you or I, but since you have to prove it to the student loan people to get your debt cancelled, proving it to the IRS will be easy.

I suspect that once this gets fully implemented, the student loan people will not even be reporting the cancelled loans to the IRS if you meet the requirements, so this information is probably useless.

**My Advice**: Make sure that if you get student loans cancelled due to disability and receive a 1099C for it that you properly exclude it from income. Do NOT just ignore the 1099C!

# If You Have a Hobby That Makes Money

The Trump Tax Law screwed you:

A lot of people have no idea that you have to report any income that you make, even if it is from a hobby or enterprise that you are not trying to make a profit on. Before the Trump Tax Law, you were allowed to deduct your expenses, but only up to the amount of income you made. You still didn't get that great of a deal, because you deducted them as an itemized deduction subject to the 2% of income limitations, which meant you both had to have enough deductions to make itemizing worth it, AND, even if you had enough to itemize, the 2% floor meant you didn't get all the benefit from your deductions.

As if that was not bad enough, making you claim all your income but not giving deductions the same treatment, now you can't deduct ANY hobby expenses. The entire 2% of income category of deductions was eliminated.

The only positive side is that the vast majority of hobbies do not make that much income, and the old limits to deductions means that the change is unlikely to have a dramatic effect on most people's bottom line. But it is still BS.

**My Advice**: If you get a 1099MISC with a number in box 7 for doing some side work unrelated to your job, especially if it is interesting or fun, you can use the Hobby Rule to claim the income as a Hobby vice as a business. This subjects it to a lower amount of taxes, though you get no deductions. It also simplifies the tax return.

# College Savings Plans and Elementary and Secondary School

This section is about state-run 529 college savings plans. They have different names in different states, but, basically, they allow people to put money into tax deferred accounts for a designated person, for their later use to pay college expenses. If you take the money out for qualified college expenses, you do not pay taxes on the withdrawal.

The Trump Tax Law allows you to withdraw up to $10,000 per year, per student to pay for tuition related expenses at public, private or religious elementary and secondary (middle and high school) educational institutions.

A lot of states allow you to get a deduction for contributing to these accounts (almost always the one setup by your state of residence) and many have no limitation on the timing of withdrawals. This means that it is possible to contribute money that you have already earmarked for these kinds of expenses, get a state tax deduction, and then pull it out and spend it as planned. I would suggest getting professional advice before doing this.

The tax law changes passed with the December 2019 budget bills included a change to 529 plans as well. You can now use up to $10,000 from 529 accounts, per year, to pay off student loans. You cannot deduct interest paid this way, but you can use the same trick discussed above to get a state tax deduction on money you were using to pay student loans anyway. The loss of the Federal interest deduction in favor of a state tax deduction makes the math on this one harder.

**My Advice**: If you are paying student loans, sending a kid to college, or sending a child to private school, using a tax professional to take advantage of the loopholes discussed above can be worth a pretty penny. There is really no downside to funneling money through a 529 plan (when your state gives you a deduction for it) for private school, but student loans and college are MUCH more complicated. We covered the weirdness for student loans, but college is even crazier. Most people with 529 plans blissfully use this money for college without realizing that, in many cases they are sacrificing over $10,000 in college credits over 4 years for a piddly amount of tax savings. I am going to include a blog post I wrote on this subject as the next chapter to kind of explain how this works.

# The $10,000 Question for Students and Parents

The American Opportunity Credit is worth up to $10,000 over four years of undergraduate schooling. Getting this right is a HUGE deal...like $10,000 huge. So, read on!

In many cases, where students or parents are paying for school, or using student loans for expenses, the credit is straightforward, and the choices limited. I will briefly discuss the one main choice in this area, but the real purpose of this article is about students getting scholarships or using 529 plan assets to pay for school. Their choices can be more complicated, and the dollar amounts lost due to mistakes are staggering.

First, let us talk about the easy scenario. If you pay all or most of your tuition, books, and course related fees out of pocket or with loans, and you meet the other qualifications discussed later, your only real decision is which years to use the credit. You see, you can take the credit a maximum of 4 tax years, but most students will spend 5 or more tax years in school (because they start in the fall of one year and finish in spring of the fifth tax year, even when only in school 4 years). If expenses are extremely low in the first year, it might make sense to wait and take the credit in the second year to maximize benefits. This is kinda like playing tax-chicken - waiting to swerve until the last second hoping you spend more time in school and pay more for it in later years. It is not easy. I generally advise taking it at the earliest opportunity unless the dollar amounts are VERY low, or the undergraduate experience will be long - such as several years of Community College before going full bore into a bachelor's degree.

Now let's talk about the 2nd scenario - scholarships or college savings plan (529 or other tax deferred education account - names vary by state) plan money: Obviously, if you can get college paid for with your college savings plan or a scholarship you should just do it and not be out of pocket for any money, right? Sure, you don't get an education credit on your taxes, but your college is paid for, so, Even-Steven, right?

Not so fast. The American Opportunity Credit (I will use AOTC from now on) gets you $2,500 for the first $4,000 of qualified education expenses. That is a 62.5% return on your money. To make things even more crazy, the first $2,000 of expenses come back DOLLAR for DOLLAR! Spend $2,000, get $2,000 - that is a 100% return! So the first $2,000 is MAGIC, but the next $2,000 ain't bad either.

I'm going to refer to all tax advantaged college savings plans as 529's from now on.

For 529 plans, it's easy: if you meet the requirements for the AOTC summarized at the end of this article, there will rarely be a situation where you don't win by paying $4,000 out of pocket and NOT using the 529 plan for that portion of education expenses. Run the numbers both ways before deciding, just to make sure (a tax pro might be useful). Unless you are in a very high tax bracket (in which case you probably don't meet the income limits for the AOTC anyway) the tax credit will exceed the tax benefits you get from using 529 plan money. Keep in mind, even though you are paying for college out of pocket instead of using 529 plan money which you had already saved, the 529 plan money is STILL THERE. It is still yours. You can use it for later years of school, transfer it to another student, or just take it out and pay the penalties and taxes. These taxes will ALWAYS be less than the maximum AOTC on $4,000 - a LOT less, since you only pay taxes and penalties on 529 plan EARNINGS, not the whole amount.

For scholarships and Pell Grants, which are generally tax free, you can include some or all of them as the recipient's income in order to allow the AOTC to be taken. Not all scholarships have this option – they must not be limited to tuition only. Just add it to your wages line on your Form 1040 with "SCH" on the line in front of it (you have to figure out how to make your software do this). Generally, $4,000 of scholarships claimed as taxable income, meaning it was used for "living expenses" instead of tuition, will have less taxes on it than the $2,500 in AOTC that you get.

Over 4 years, this can make you $10,000 that you wouldn't otherwise have had. It is well worth working with a professional to make sure you do it right if you aren't certain. The IRS is pretty anal about the AOTC, but that is no reason not to take it.

Here are a few more things to consider:

This chapter has nothing to do with VA or other military education benefits. If you get them, you almost never get the AOTC, except maybe on books.

The simplified formula for determining how much expenses you get AOTC for is tuition PLUS course related books and fees MINUS tax free scholarships and grants MINUS 529 type funds used. This amount, up to $4,000, gets you the credit. We are manipulating the 529 plan amount, and changing tax-free scholarships and grants to make them taxable, to change the final number to maximize education credits.

Make sure you include the income and credits on the right tax return: parent or student. Mostly, the 529 plan and taxable scholarship money will be on the student's return, and the credit will be on the parent's. Unless a student is over the age of 24 or has job income that equals more than half of their support, or is fully emancipated, the AOTC will be far better on the parent's return (and may not be allowed on the student's). If there is a choice, do the returns side by side to make sure. If you still aren't sure, talk to a pro.

If either the student or the parent is getting the Earned Income Tax Credit for having a low income and children, the inclusion of scholarship money as income can have a bigger negative effect. Run the numbers, using no AOTC, $2,000 for AOTC and $4,000 for AOTC to see which is better, and then act accordingly.

Here are the simplified requirements for the AOTC (don't rely on them for final decisions, these are just here to let you know if this entire article might be useless to you):

For the 2020 tax year, if you file Married Filing Jointly, your AOTC is limited if your AGI hits $160,000 and is gone at $180,000. Other filing statuses the numbers are $80,000 to $90,000.

The student must be going at least half time
The student can't have been convicted of a felony drug offense
You get AOTC a maximum of 4 tax years per student

The AOTC is for undergraduate work, so you can't have completed a 4 year degree (you can get AOTC for graduate work you do in the same year you finish your bachelor's degree - TAX SAVING SECRET)

They must be attending an eligible education institution for an eligible degree or certificate (most 2 or 4 year schools will qualify, others, double check yourself.

For more great information designed for College Students, Check out The Short Cheap Tax Book for Students

# Tuition and Fees Deduction

While we're talking about education, let's talk about another Zombie Deduction: The Tuition and Fees deduction was reinstated for 2019 AND 2018 with the budget bill passed late in 2019. Now it has been reinstated for 2020 but looks like it might finally be dead after that.

The below was copied and edited from Everyday Taxes 2019/2020

The Tuition and Fees Deduction is usually the least beneficial of the education benefits; you get a deduction from income instead of a tax credit. It is an "above the line" deduction, which means it improves your taxes whether you itemize or not and may reduce your AGI for figuring other limitations. The expenses that you can deduct for this deduction are virtually the same as the American Opportunity Credit (AOC), except that books and course-related fees are only included if they MUST be paid directly to the education institution as a condition of enrollment. One big caveat on all this education stuff is that the AOC and the Lifetime Learning Credit (LLC) have no effect on state taxes. This deduction often does, so when determining whether this is better than the LLC or AOC, make sure to check your state taxes as well. Here are the details:

a. If college expenses do not exceed scholarships and tax advantaged sources, you get nothing.

b. If you are not attending at least half-time, you can still get this deduction.

c. If the student has been convicted of a felony drug offense, you still get this deduction.

d. The student has to be attending an eligible school with or without the intention of getting a degree or credential, which includes virtually every accredited postsecondary (post high school) institution. This can even include colleges outside the U.S. if they are eligible to participate in the U.S. Federal Student Aid program. The college can tell you if they are eligible. This includes truck driving school, welding school and other non-degree attaining schools.

e. You cannot be filing Married Filing Separately.

f. If your AGI exceeds $160,000 (MFJ) or $80,000 (HH or Single) you cannot get this deduction.

g. You can deduct a maximum of $4,000 if your income is less than $130,000 (MFJ) or $65,000 (Single or HH). If your income is between $130,000 and $160,000 (MFJ) or between $65,000 and $80,000 (HH or Single) you can deduct $2,000. This is per tax return, not per person.

h. Calculate your expenses for Form 8917. This number will be tuition and course related fees (if required to be paid to the institution as discussed above) minus tax-free scholarships, grants and tax advantaged funding sources. This is the number you will use when filling out Form 8917 or entering data in your software program.

**My Advice**: This is rarely of significant benefit to anyone. Not one of my 2019 tax clients could have used this to improve their 2018 tax return. That said, if you or your child were in college in 2018, check your return to see if this would have helped, especially if they did not qualify for the American Opportunity Credit.

# Entertainment Deduction Changes

Essentially all deductions for entertainment expenses have been eliminated. This applies to both businesses and employees (all employee business expense deductions were eliminated with the rest of the deductions subject to the 2% of Adjusted Gross Income limit). All expenses for any activity generally considered to be entertainment, amusement, or recreation, as well as membership dues to any club organized for business, pleasure, recreation or other social purposes are now not deductible. Entertainment facilities are also not deductible.

The only expense that sort of fell in this category that survived, was the deduction for 50% of meals provided for employees or food and beverage expenses paid in conjunction with operating their business.

This was clarified in 2019 to say that meals where the taxpayer is present and that are not extravagant are still 50% deductible for current or potential business clients, customers, consultants, or other business contacts.

For 2021 and 2022 the meal deduction has been relaxed and made deductible at 100%

**My Advice**: Make sure for meals with clients that you note on the receipt who was present, what was discussed, and how it was intended to improve your business.

# Do Not Believe What You Hear About Tax Laws

Unless you hear about it from a competent professional that you trust, it is very likely to be crap information. Government websites are usually reliable. Big financial publications (Kiplinger's for example) are pretty good. Newspapers and broadcast news are terrible. Blogs (other than mine), Facebook posts, Reddit, friends, neighbors...all useless. Competent tax professionals are the only people you should trust for sure.

You can't even trust IRS employees. Believe it or not, if you get an answer from the IRS over the phone, and it's wrong, it's still on you. You need it in writing.

I wrote myself a note to list all the stupid things about taxes I have heard, but there is just no room, and no way to pick a winner.

**My Advice**: Re-read what I just wrote ;)

# Some Things to Know About How Changes Will be Implemented

The purpose of this chapter is to basically say, "Just because laws were passed, does not mean we really know what they mean, and we might not know all the nitty gritty details for YEARS!"

What is passed is the LAW. Modifications to the Code of Federal Regulations 26 - IRS Code (though the law is written like an edit to the code - insert here, replace here, etc.)

The IRS will need to interpret it, and then issue proposed new REGULATIONS, which will be commented on, modified, and finally approved. The Code and Regulations are the rules that must be followed.

Then they will update their PUBLICATIONS, FORMS and INSTRUCTIONS - that is how most people figure out what to do on their return, and part of how tax software is written.

Then people will do things on their taxes that the IRS doesn't like and think violates the law. Some will go to court, and rulings will be made. The IRS will win some and the taxpayer will win others. Once something is litigated, we will finally have confidence what it means. This can take YEARS.

Bottom line, for many areas of the law, we will not have a true idea how they will be implemented and interpreted for quite some time (other areas are obvious).

**My Advice**: There is not a lot actionable here, except to say that if you take a questionable or aggressive interpretation of the new tax laws, it is a good idea to know how much benefit you received, and, if it is significant, set it aside for three years just to be safe.

# Selling Your Home

As promised, I am going to briefly discuss the rules for not having to pay taxes on any profit when you sell your home.

Before that, I am going to remind you that if you LOSE money selling your home, you do not get to deduct the loss, which makes being able to exclude the gain seem fair.

So, if you owned AND lived in the home for 2 of the last 5 years, never rented it out and never ran a business out of the home, you can exclude up to $250,000 of profit on the sale of your home ($500,000 if filing MFJ). You DO NOT have to reinvest the money in a new home. VERY basically, if the selling price minus what you paid for it is less than $250,000 ($500,000 MFJ) then you pay no taxes on the sale. Generally, at closing, one of the papers you sign will attest that you meet this exclusion, and they will not even report the sale to the IRS!

If you do not meet the times, but had to move for an unexpected reason, you might be able to get a portion of the exclusion. See a professional. If you used it for business or rented it out, see a professional.

**My Advice**: The next person you hear who says you have to reinvest the money in a new home within two years, slap them. Actually, don't hit them but do correct them. That hasn't been the law for decades!

# Personal Residence Cancelled Debt Exclusion

The ability to exclude from income cancelled debt that was secured by your personal residence was reinstated for 2019 AND 2018 with the late December 2019 tax law changes. If you had a house foreclosed on in either of those years, this applies to you. The details below were copied and edited from Everyday Taxes 2019/2020. This is another Zombie Provision that I do not expect to go away permanently, though it is currently not applicable to 2020 and beyond. If the COVID-19 downturn starts affecting the housing market, you can bet Congress will reinstate this so fast it will make our heads spin!

**BIG UPDATE**: The law has been extended through 2025!

You can exclude canceled debt on the foreclosure of your primary home. It has to be your personal residence at the time of foreclosure. There is some debate on this as to whether you need to be living in the home the day of foreclosure, but most take the reasonable position that if you leave the home due to imminence of foreclosure, you can exclude it as personal residence. The 2 out of 5-year rule for excluding gain does not apply here, though the rules can make you think it does. The definition of "personal residence" from that part of the code applies, not the time rules, so make sure you can defend the position that it was your residence at the time of foreclosure. If you moved out and stopped making the payments for a year, or converted it to a rental for a while, this probably does not apply, but talk to a professional just to make sure. There are detailed restrictions and limitations on this, so it makes sense to check with a tax professional in any case.

Keep Reading:

You may also receive a Form 1099-A, but not always. The 1099-A represents the transfer of your house to the mortgage company and is treated as if you sold it. Many banks totally suck at sending this paperwork, and often you will get a 1099-C and not the 1099-A, but you should report the sale. The good news is that as long as you don't use the property for business, it's generally a tax neutral situation. You report the property as sold on Schedule D, as a personal residence. If you owned and lived in the home for 2 of the last 5 years, never rented it to someone, and never used it for business, you can exclude $250,000 of gain ($500,000 if MFJ). You will include the date purchased, date sold (from the 1099-A or 1099-C, the price you paid [basis] and the price sold [Fair Market Value from the 1099-A or 1099-C]). Make sure you indicate it as personal residence property. Your software should exclude the gain as appropriate, and not allow a loss if that is the result. You may need to see a professional for help on this.

**My Advice**: 1099A forms and 1099C forms come notoriously late for these events. If you are foreclosed on, ASK if one is coming. Also, they tend to be wrong, so make sure yours is correct. Don't panic if you get them (especially for 2019 and before) and seek out assistance to make sure you don't pay taxes on it, or pay the minimum amount.

# Residential Energy Credits

The Non-business Energy Property Credit was reinstated for 2019 AND 2018 with the late December 2019 Tax Law Changes. Energy Credits are like Uber Zombie Provisions. What qualifies, when and why changes CONSTANTLY. The law has been extended AGAIN through 2021. Always ask someone knowledgeable on the subject if you are doing anything that improves the energy efficiency of your home. Do NOT rely on what the salesman says – especially if they are selling Solar. They are incredibly misinformed at best, and liars at worst. The below was copied and edited from Everyday Taxes 2019/2020.

1. The Non-business Energy Property Credit is 10% of qualifying costs, with a LIFETIME maximum credit for all costs of $500.
2. The LIFETIME maximum credit for windows is $200 (this is inclusive, not in addition to the $500 limit; if you take $200 for windows, you only have $300 for the rest of your life for other things).
3. They are subject to AGI limitations.
4. The credit is available for insulation, exterior doors, windows, skylights and roofs that are SPECIFICALLY designed to reduce heat loss or gain.
5. It also applies to water heaters, heating systems, and air conditioners that are near the most efficient available at the time of installation.
6. The instructions for the current year form will identify the standards to be met, but the manufacturer or installer can also tell you. They must provide, and you must maintain, documentation to prove that it meets these standards. I recommend that you make the contractor or salesman SHOW you the documentation and proof that it meets the standards. Energy Star does not mean crap—these items have to be really high quality (and generally more expensive than non-qualified items).
7. If you share the house with someone other than your spouse, you get the credit based on what you paid, and the maximum is applied based on the percentage paid by each occupant.

8. If you and your spouse have separate main homes, there are extra hoops to jump through and you will need a bit of professional help to be safe.

**My Advice**: Things to investigate and save documentation for, even if the credit currently is not allowed are doors, windows, insulation, solar, wind, electric car chargers, HVAC units and hot water heaters. Not all of these are under this credit, but credits exist from time to time on all of them. Save receipts and details for all of these documenting the cost and the energy efficiency ratings

# Mortgage Insurance Premium Deduction

The Mortgage Insurance Premium deduction was reinstated for 2019 AND 2018 with the late December 2019 tax law changes. AND in December 2020 it was applied to 2020 and 2021!

The below was copied and edited from Everyday Taxes 2019/2020.

Mortgage insurance premiums (including VA, FHA and USDA funding fees) may be deductible. You can generally find these on the Master Settlement Statement or your 1098 Form. Here are the details:

1. The home must have been purchased after December 31, 2006.
2. The deduction is decreased by 10% for every $1000 AGI exceeds $100,000 ($500 and $50,000 for MFS).
3. Must be for first or second home.
4. Prepaid insurance premiums must be spread out over 7 years or the life of the loan, except for insurance provided by the VA or Rural Housing Authority.

## My Advice:

1. If you bought a new home in 2018 or 2019, check your Master Settlement Statement for a VA Funding Fee, FHA/USDA Funding Fee or any other mortgage insurance premiums.
2. Check your 1098 forms for 2018 and 2019 and see if these premiums are on them.
3. Check your monthly mortgage statement to see if you paid these premiums and they were not reported on your 1098 forms.

# Retirement and 529 Plan Account Changes

This section is a summary of the late December 2019 tax law changes affecting retirement and 529 plans. It does not include the relief provided for specific disasters including Coronavirus. These are permanent changes. Some of these are covered in more detail elsewhere.

1. Starting in 2020 you can contribute to Traditional IRA's even if you are older than 70 and a half.

2. For people not already required to make Required Minimum Distributions, the starting age has been raised from 70 and a half to 72. As an aside, remember that per the Coronavirus Tax Bill, 2020 Required Minimum Distributions are NOT required. 2021 and later still are.

3. A new exception to the 10% penalty for early retirement account withdrawals was created for 2020 and later. You can exclude the penalty on up to $5000 withdrawn within one year after the birth or adoption of a child. This applies to both 401k's and IRA's.

4. You can use up to $10,000 from a 529 plan to pay student loans without penalty or inclusion in income. You cannot deduct student loan interest paid this way.

5. Requirements to contribute to IRA's and 401k's have been relaxed. These include redefining income for graduate students, allowing part time workers to contribute to 401k's, and making difficulty of care payments eligible compensation for IRA's.

6. IRA's inherited in 2020 and later by non-spouses need to be withdrawn within 10 years. There are a few exceptions for minors and the disabled.

# My Other Books

If you like this book, you should check out my others:

Everyday Taxes 2019/2020 covers over 70 life situations with detailed information and advice in English. It is my most comprehensive (and expensive) tax book but is indispensable no matter how you file. The idea is to be able to look up a chapter on what is happening in your life, see the effect on your taxes, and then take action to improve or mitigate the effect. I am including a chapter list on the last page of this book page. The 2020/2021 version will be out in June of 2020.

The Short Cheap Tax Book for Everyone is 50 plus pieces of advice that EVERYONE needs to know. Some of it is obvious (though ignored), some of it is obscure, but all of it is important (A small amount has been copied into this book).

The Short Cheap tax Book for Students has a ton of tax, financial and life advice for High School or College students to get their financial life started right.

The Short Cheap Math Book is a short, snarky primer of math from numbers to basic Algebra.

Kirk's First Crappy NANO Book: The Sword is my first try at fiction. It isn't actually crappy, I just called it that because I promised to publish the books I wrote during National Novel Writing Month no matter how poorly edited they ended up being. This one came out pretty good.

I have several others, and am working on more, so keep an eye on my author page:

amazon.com/author/kirkea

## Review and Share This Book

If you found this book helpful, the best thing you can do for me is to give it a glowing review on Amazon and tell everyone about it.

Also consider buying my other books – at the very least The Short Cheap Tax Book for Everyone.

# List of Chapters/Topics from Everyday Taxes

38. I am Living with Someone Who Helps Pay my Bills
39. I am Supporting my Parents
40. I am Supporting an Adult Relative or Friend
41. I am Supporting a Minor Who is Not My Child
42. Someone Claimed my Child!
43. My Tax Return Got Rejected by the IRS!
44. I (or my Spouse or Child) am Going to College
45. I Have to Pay for Things for my Job
46. I Tele-Commute
47. I Work Overseas
48. I Lost my Job
49. I Had to Move
50. I Sold my Home
51. I Sold my Rental Property
52. I Sold a Home that Wasn't my Primary Residence
53. I Get Tips at Work
54. I Receive Benefits from the Government
55. I Have Investments Outside of Work
56. I Have (or Want to Have) Tax Sheltered Investments (IRA's)
57. I Want to Take Money out of my IRA or 401k
58. I Had Debt Written Off by the Company I Owe Money To
59. I Lost my House (Foreclosure, Short Sale or Bankruptcy)
60. I am Retired (or Thinking about it)
61. I am Retiring from the Military (Here Are Some Warnings)
62. I am Receiving Social Security (or Thinking about It)
63. I am Receiving an Annuity or Pension
64. I am Paying on Student Loans
65. I am Changing Jobs
66. What the Hell is Alternative Minimum Tax?
67. I Sell Amway, Mary Kay, etc.
68. I'm an Independent Contractor or I Got a Form 1099-MISC
69. I Drive for UBER (or other cab like business)
70. I am (or will be) a Real Estate Agent
71. I am an Artist (Tailored to Painters)
72. I am Renting out my Former Home
73. What about the Affordable Care Act (Obamacare)
74. I Get Health Insurance Through the Healthcare Marketplace
75. I Do Not Have Health Insurance
76. State by State Tax Guide for Military